THE DIVINE PLAN
and its realization

by S. Van Mierlo

ISBN: 978-1-78364-590-9

The Open Bible Trust

www.obt.org.uk

THE DIVINE PLAN
and its realization

Contents

ABOUT THIS BOOK

This book is not a commentary. It is an exposition of the Scriptures based on a detailed, systematic examination of the Word of God, using what the author describes as the "scientific approach:" an objective examination of a document without preconceived ideas and excluding the human element, or bias, as far as possible. The Scriptures are explained by the Scriptures, rather than by what commentators may have said about this document.

The author presents the steps which he pursued in his objective examination of the Bible, taking the reader with him along the path which he himself followed. It happens that this "scientific" approach is precisely that advocated by Dr. Bullinger in his book *How to Enjoy the Bible*. In his Introduction, page xv, he quotes Bishop Butler who has "pointed the way," saying that "the only way to study the Word of God is the way in which physical science is studied."

Trained and practicing as a scientist, the author decided one day to examine the Bible to see if it was indeed a "special" book, different from all others. This he followed through, and Bible research became a first priority from that time on. He became co-editor of a monthly magazine in the Dutch language, Uit de Schriften (Out of the Scriptures), with Mr. Pauptit of Holland. Meanwhile he came to know and highly prize the outstanding works of two eminent pioneers in the Truth: Dr. E.W. Bullinger and Mr. Ch. H. Welch.

Over the years he contributed a number of articles and monographs, lectured in various seminars of religious orders in Europe, and wrote a number of books during the period from the early 1930s to 1960 before he fell asleep in Christ.

Among the author's works is a series of five books which form a logical sequence in which the present book occupies third place. A synopsis of these books is given in the last Appendix to this volume.

The author, S. Van Mierlo, never claimed to be infallible, encouraged students not to put their trust in men's writings, but rather rest their faith on **the power of the Word of God**, and invited readers' comments and critiques. He relentlessly applied the instructions to divide rightly, to distinguish the things that differ and to the best of his ability labored to be "a workman that needeth not to be ashamed, comparing spiritual things with spiritual," all things being done to the glory of God.

This work was translated from the French by the author's son, who must accept the blame for those passages which might have been rendered more clearly! The help of many sincere believers, both within and outside the family, is hereby gratefully acknowledged. (The Lord knows who they are.)

John Van Mierlo

California, October 1989

> For by the grace given me, I say to every one of you: Do not think of yourself more highly than you ought, but rather think of yourself with sober judgment, in accordance with the measure of faith God has given you.

Rom. 12:3 (NIV)

> But to each of us grace has been given as Christ apportioned it.

Eph. 4:7 (NIV)

INTRODUCTION

In our work, *Science, Reason and Faith,* we have examined the question of the existence of God. We have endeavored to demonstrate that is is more reasonable to believe in the existence of a "supra-personal" God than not to believe in one. Often, a conscious or unconscious repugnance to surrendering our independence drives us (through feeling rather than reason) to doubt God's existence.

In our book, *The Divine Revelation*, we have discussed problems relating to the inspiration and interpretation of Scripture. These two studies basically constitute an introduction to this present work, which is the result of a methodical examination of the Bible, aimed at providing a summary of its contents from the special viewpoint of the realization of the "Divine Plan."

It happens that certain of our conclusions differ from those of other theologians and believers. Thus, some may claim that we are merely increasing opportunities for disagreement and division. However, our intention is not to present "something new," rather, we wish, at all costs, to better understand the Truth, and to clear up some of the current confusion. We have undertaken this study to arrive at personal convictions concerning a number of questions, and we hope this work may prove helpful to others also.

The scope of our efforts in fact far exceeds the defense of this or that point of view. It concerns above all the exposition and application of a method, and the setting up of a personal attitude which, we believe, enables a man a good will to perceive the truth wherever it is found.

To understand this method, consider for example the contrast which exists between progress achieved in the physical sciences versus that in philosophy and theology.[1]

In the physical sciences we have witnessed considerable development, with major impact on industry and the material things of life. A unique "system" has been developed which is strictly systematic, open, and infinitely perfectible, through collaboration among scientists everywhere; a single path is followed which seems to lead to the truth.

On the other hand, in philosophy and theology, there is little agreement or tangible progress. Violent antagonisms often exist between different "systems" which divide thinkers and believers. Divergent paths are followed which must, in general, lead away from the truth.

Why this startling difference? Because physical sciences have continued to follow a "natural" method. It is the same method which permits a child's rapid development in early life, to become aware of the real world of which he is a part. Taking a closer look at this method – which the scientist interprets as a "scientific method" – we note that this method is based, more or less consciously, on the following principles:

1. One accepts, through a preliminary faith, the existence of a real "whole," without any intrinsic contradictions, which is basically understandable. Nothing is eliminated *a priori*, nothing is isolated.

2. One becomes acquainted with the elements of this "whole" without preconceived ideas, without intervention of biased feelings (love or repugnance).
3. The preceding implies both humility and an invincible love of the truth, which lead to a sacrifice of self, to not considering oneself as center of the universe, to not measuring everything by one's own mediocre standard.

4. One thus follows the "method" of faith and love – but a fully reasonable faith which uses all the spiritual faculties. There is no question of an unjustifiable credulity. Nor is this method solely "intellectual," it involves the whole of our being. It is a method that is lived to the fullest extent.

When the application of such a method or attitude has enabled us to progress a little, we will understand why this method of faith and love is successful: it is because this attitude implies that we humble our self before God, that we do not resist the Spirit Who wants to regenerate and enlighten us, turn us into perfect men, give us perfect Life. Then, we also understand that the usual methods cannot succeed fully because in those cases we rely on our own strengths which are in themselves insufficient to reach the Truth, to really progress, to acquire this Life. There exists in those false methods a certain self-centeredness which – although it may be unconscious – prevents the development of our being, paralyses us, and tends to annihilate us because we are separated from the Source.

Why has similar progress not been realized in other sciences, and especially not in philosophy and theology? We believe it is because here, to a much stronger degree, two contrary influences intervene: one derived from external sources, evil in the world, and one from a personal source, evil within us.

Thus we believe that the physical sciences have succeeded because, in their limited domain, they have consistently followed the "natural" method, the method of *faith and love*.

To be fair, we must also recognize that the physical domain is more accessible to man, whose spirit is "attuned to matter," than are the domains of philosophy and theology.

Having had the privilege to be trained in scientific disciplines, and having observed that the "natural" or "scientific" method leads to rapid progress, we tried to apply this method to the study of the Bible. Starting as an agnostic, and having belatedly come into contact with the Scriptures, we nevertheless did not reject *a priori* that this Book might be Divine revelation. We wished to remain "scientific" and to entertain the possibility that the Bible might be different from all that man has produced. And yet everything impelled against such a concept: external influences, education, native egocentrism.

A preliminary examination indicated that often the reproaches and accusations concerned only certain *interpretations* of the text, but not necessarily the Bible itself. Besides, this Book seemed to provide the elements of a complete system, one part of which explaining the other. Why not, we pondered, consider it as a whole, as it is, without judging it by another system? Could it present a better system or a more complete system than the others?

If one wants to apply the scientific method to a scrutiny of the Bible, one must therefore:

- o Have faith (or at least a provisional faith which is equivalent to what the man of science calls "a working hypothesis") in the unity and the truthfulness of the Book.

o Have a love of the truth, the whole truth, and thus be ready to sacrifice if necessary one's own convictions and all traditions of human origin.

We have explained at some length our predisposition to a preliminary faith in the whole Scriptures, in our work *The Divine Revelation*. In our opinion, modern criticism has committed a basic error. It has erred not by criticizing, per se (i.e., by examination using discursive intelligence, by reasoning, by eliminating errors of interpretation). Rather, the mistake resides first of all, in assuming that science is based on the method: study, then faith; and second, in applying that method to the study of the Bible. The true scientific method, on the other hand, may be summarized this way:

1. Overall faith in the unity and intelligibility of the subject being studied.

2. Study, led by a love of the truth, without *a priori* judgments or beliefs.

3. Development of a particular faith about particular details.

Modern criticism has lost sight of the first item and hence is violently fighting a preliminary faith in the unity and veracity of the Bible. This kind of criticism would be correct if it had been proven that the attitude towards a faith which accepts the verbal inspiration of the text was untenable to an enlightened and reasonable man. But this has never been proven. On the contrary, as we have tried to show in *The Divine Revelation*, not only does the text resist all human criticism, but it is always confirmed by *the facts*, even though it has appeared, during certain periods, to be condemned by *theories*. Hence we submit, after a lengthy analysis, that where certainty of conclusion is concerned rather than provisional theory, thought and science always confirm the unity and the absolute veracity of the text, a phenomenon which does not occur with any other document.

Having arrived at this significant result, one is led to study the text and to interpret it correctly, explaining Scripture by Scripture, just as the scientist studies and interprets the data from Nature. By applying the scientific method consistently, one may construct a "Science of the Scripture" which continually draws closer to the Truth. If researchers follow the method we have outlined always permitting the Truth to correct their ideas, they may come close to unanimity.

This is the method we have tried to follow, and the reader will not be surprised to see us sacrificing certain traditional tenets and human interpretations. We can sympathize with the reader when he is led to abandon some concept dearly held and which may have been a blessing to him, because we also have been frequently obliged to give up our own convictions. But is not the Truth even more precious? Sometimes one may feel that we are losing certain values, but then one begins to realize the enormous benefits acquired by abandoning that which is partial truth and which may be a major stumbling block in one's spiritual life.

After these general observations, we wish to explain certain aspects of our attitude (in particular, to some modern theologians). In our work *The Divine Revelation*, we have tried to refute the objection that a preliminary faith in Scripture's infallible authority contradicts the exigencies of the spirit; such theologians oppose the "spirit" of the text to the "letter," they also oppose spiritual life to what they call theological intellectualism or "biblicism."

If God is the Author of the Bible, there cannot be any valid objection to accepting as sovereign authority that which He wants us to know; it is only reasonable that we bow to His Word. The exigencies of the spirit cannot consist in rejecting the Truth. This "letter," while it is addressed to our intelligence, serves only as intermediary. For it speaks about spiritual things, and intellectual acceptance must or should accompany the personal experience of that which is expressed and understood. It is possibly true that some have given too much emphasis to the letter only, but this is not a good reason to sacrifice the letter and retain only the spirit.

The letter is adapted to our condition of fallen man, whose spirit is clouded and incapable to seize directly the Truth. God acts within us but does not reveal everything to us individually This is a situation similar to that in the physical world where our spirit is obliged to use our senses as intermediary. By our own conscience we are incapable of reaching any but the vaguest concept of the truth. The Spirit enlightens our spirit to enable us to understand, not a revelation which would be strictly personal, but that which He has revealed once for all in a precise manner to certain chosen persons and also by means of a written document. We do not worship a book, but the Word of God which is expressed in it with the help of a human language.

A pure intellectual knowledge of the "letter" is evidently not sufficient, but an intellectual acceptance of this "letter" is indispensable to arriving at a knowledge of what God has revealed, and to loving the Lord in more than a vague manner. Our degree of love depends upon how well we know the One loved, and the Apostle Paul himself aspired to a better knowledge of the Lord. If it is God Himself Who speaks to us with precise words which contain neither error nor contradictions, we can have an enlightened faith and be quite certain about many details.

On the other hand, if the Bible is merely a collection of fallible testimonies, of rudimentary expressions that certain men have understood through their normal "religious conscience" we can never reach certainty on specific points of Scripture. All that is left then – if one wants to remain logical – is a vague religiosity, more or less "Christian." And even so, far from brushing aside the principle of authority, the professional theologian will tend to substitute his own human authority for the supreme authority of the Word. Believers will then gather under the leadership of this human authority, individually or collectively, and the "confession of faith" of a church or a sect will replace the Scriptures.

Let us now add a few words addressed to "simple" believers. Why all these complications, these references to Science, Philosophy and Theology? Why not simply accept what the Bible teaches?

Let us avoid misunderstandings. There is, on the one hand, a simplicity which consists in not resisting the Truth, not forcing one's own ideas, but which nevertheless does not exclude thought, reason, and a certain critique. That which belongs to the sphere of the Divine is assuredly rational, and will withstand the most searching critical examination. If God acts within us through His Spirit, it is not to make us stupid. On the contrary, He acts to enlighten our spirit, our intelligence, and our reason. We must retain all our critical faculties in relation to the *interpretations* of the Word, and also to those of the "authorities."

There is thus a simplicity which accepts the Truth when it presents itself, while at the same time keeping and exercising all one's faculties of the mind. It is true that Scripture commends to us the simplicity of the child, but this is precisely that quality of which we have been speaking, and which helps us to remain receptive to the Truth. There is absolutely no question of relinquishing our reason. The Apostle Paul clearly spells this out: "Brethren, be not children in understanding: howbeit in malice be ye children, but in understanding be men." (1 Cor. 14:20).

On the other hand, there is a simplicity which is nothing but credulity, which accepts too easily even the error, which does not make an adequate effort to fully understand what God wishes to make known. The Bible itself, however, invites us to examine and to think: "I speak as to wise men: judge ye what I say." (1 Cor. 10:15). "Prove all things; hold fast that which is good. Abstain from all appearance of evil." (1 Thess. 5:21, 22). "Study to show thyself approved unto God, a workman that needeth not to be ashamed, rightly dividing the word of truth." (2 Tim. 2:15).

Undoubtedly, in many cases where important but elementary questions are involved, the text speaks clearly to those who want to listen. Any man will thus be able to learn the first stages of the way to salvation. But things become more complicated when it becomes a matter of correctly understanding a teaching a little more advanced, and when it becomes a question of institutions, ordinances, rites, social life. It is not enough to state that this or that is mentioned in the Bible; one must learn to carefully discern to whom certain words are addressed, and what time or "dispensation" is involved. God does not change, but the earthly circumstances change; God administers the world in different ways, and does not speak to the spiritual "child" as He does to the "perfect Man."

All His ordinances are not given forever to all the world. Before the flood, man was to be vegetarian; after the flood he was permitted to eat meat. The people of Israel had to observe laws and ordinances which, as such, were not strictly applicable to the Gentiles. There was a time when the Lord's disciples were ordered to take nothing with them on their journeys, not even money and especially not arms. But in another time, the Lord Himself changed those requirements. (Compare Luke 9:3 with Luke 22:35-36). The reader will often meet such distinctions in the present work. It is thus not enough to choose some text and apply it to anyone at any time. One must consider the Bible as a whole, wherein each part finds its exact place. One must therefore study, and continue to study the Scriptures.

But there is another angle to this question. The Bible expresses in ordinary human language what God wants to tell us. Thus, physical phenomena are described as man sees them unfolding; the sun rises. There is no *error* in expressing oneself this way, as long as one does not claim to describe the phenomenon objectively, as it is taking place in full reality. One understands that God "had" to use a language we could understand. This language contains many figures of speech and specially constructed phrases.

Now it is certainly true that we must understand the Bible as literally as possible – we have personally insisted on this in *The Divine Revelation*. But one can see the danger that may confront the man who does not make full use of his intelligence: he may readily take certain subjective expressions or certain figures of speech in too strictly literal a manner. One recalls the historical drama about the question of whether the earth was motionless or not: based on a too-literal interpretation of the Scriptures, it was maintained that the earth was motionless, and anyone who did not agree was condemned. Thus does the imprudent believer risk to find himself upholding an error!

We must therefore become "perfect men," not only with respect to love, but also with respect to intelligence, for God is not only Love, but also Truth. Let us then fully love the Truth – the proper object of intelligence. We must not sacrifice love to intelligence, nor the other way round. Both can only be fully realized through their mutual support.

According to fairly current concepts, one distinguishes the "old dispensation" (that of the Law covered in the Old Testament) from the "new dispensation" (that of grace, revealed in the New Testament). Our studies show that such a distinction rests on a basis of truth, but that it is not sufficient. This gives rise to problems which seem insoluble because badly posed, and Christendom is divided as a consequence. It is first of all very important to carefully examine the different ways in which God administers the world. One must also carefully distinguish between the various stages of the believer along the way of salvation. From these distinctions will arise the interpretation to be applied to many a text, and the solution of many a difficulty.

The "ages" and "dispensations" have been studied by many serious authors, especially in the Anglo-Saxon world. But the hardest problem in this context is that concerning the times which follow the crucifixion: the period covered by the Acts of the Apostles, and the present period. Now, it happens that all our concepts relating to the notions of "Church," organization, ordinances, rites and all that concerns social relations of the believer, depend upon the solution one gives to this problem. This fundamental question does not appear to have been examined with sufficient care and objectivity by the theologians; from this come the radical differences between Churches and sects.

The solution which we present herein gradually defined itself, as with a scientific problem, with help from the studies of various persons and following the scientific method we have already outlined. We wish to mention particularly pioneers such as Dr. E. W. Bullinger and Mr. Charles H. Welch.

BEFORE THE AGES

The Greek Text reads, in 2 Tim. 1:9, "pro chronon aionion," which translates to: "before the times of the ages".[2]

Genesis introduces us into creation and time. The "beginning" of Gen. 1:1 is that of creation. But before and beyond all creation, including space and time, there is God: God "**IS**" (see Heb. 11:6, Greek "estin" (is); also Ex. 3:14 and John 8:58). He is Spirit, Love, Truth, Justice, Will, Freedom. He is completely incomprehensible to us except in what He has willed to reveal to us about Himself.

Thus we know that, although perfect and One in Himself, we have to distinguish in Him three "modes of being:" the Father, His Image,[3] and the Spirit. The Image of God was later revealed to us and was named "JHVH" (Yahweh or Jehovah),[4] "the Angel of the Lord",[5] the "Son." After He divested Himself of His glory (Phil. 2:6), the Son appeared as an ordinary man, named Jesus in His humiliation. It was the Christ announced by the prophets. The Son is God,[6] He is above all creation,[7] by Him all things consist.[8] All things were created by Him and for Him (Rom. 11:36; 1 Cor. 8:6; Col. 1:16; Heb. 2:10). He also prepared the ages (Heb. 1:2, where "aionas" is translated "worlds"). The whole of creation subsists in Him, all life, all "beings" consist in Him (Col. 1:17; Heb. 1:3; Acts 17:28).

Before the "beginning" of Genesis, therefore, there is the "beginning" of John 1:1: "In the beginning was the Word". Before the world came into being, the Son was in glory with the Father (John 17:5). Before the creation and the ages, there was a promise of life (Tit. 1:2), grace was prepared (2 Tim. 1:9), and wisdom was ordained unto our glory (1 Cor. 2:7).

The Son has been Mediator not only to create, but to bring His creature unto the glory of the Father. Had there been neither fall nor sin, He would not have had to divest Himself of His glory, take the form of a servant, humble Himself and become obedient unto death, even the death of the cross (Phil. 2:7, 8). Divine life was in Him (1 John 5:11), and He could have communicated it fully to the creature through perfect communion because all was created for Him (Col. 1:16; Rom. 11:36) God would then have been "all in all." Creation, mortal and corruptible by nature, would have been brought to immortality and incorruptibility. But the sin of the creature intervened,[9] and impeded (but did not prevent) the accomplishment of God's purposes. When these purposes will be realized, the humiliated "Jesus" will not only be supremely exalted, as He is now already (Phil 2:9), but He will be fully reintegrated into His state of Image of God. The ages will end when the final goal will have been reached, to the glory of the Father and the Son. He cannot *remain* Mediator, His work must one day be accomplished.

THE BEGINNING OF CREATION

God creates through love. Nothing constrains Him. God does not only create "things," but also more or less free and intelligent beings, worthy of their Creator. He wills that these creatures accede freely to the fulness of His blessings and of His love. In a certain sense, the existence of these free creatures is one of the proofs of the existence of God.

Creation does not proceed from "nothing," but from Him.[10] But not as an emanation, however. Creation is evidently not God, but originates from God Who subsists without change. To say that God wants a free creature is to say that He wants it fully: the aim of God is to bring, without constraint, the creature – who has no existence in itself – into full communion with Him. God wants to be, finally, "all in all," 1 Cor. 15:28.

Here we perceive a way of salvation for the creature. But, we repeat, this "way" will have to be followed freely, for God does not treat the creature as a "thing." It is thus the creature who, by means of what God renders it capable of doing, must reach its goal: to acquire life and to identify itself with God. Any constraint would diminish its freedom, so tending to annihilate it as a free and intelligent creature and thus preventing the realization of the goal. Any progress in its communion with God increases its freedom and its "being." To God's love must respond the love of the creature.

The creature must thus become conscious of its state, of the worth accorded to it by God, of its destiny.

Through its freedom (though relative), the intelligent creature is not constrained in its thinking or its actions. It can, up to a point, resist Divine grace and Divine will, i.e. that which is absolutely "good." Any good use of its freedom increases its communion with God, renders it freer with respect to evil. And conversely.[11]

Another question now arises: how has the creature used its freedom? We can answer that basing ourselves on two things: 1. What we know about visible creation, including ourselves; 2. What God has said about it in His Word.

Well, although our natural faculties enable us to see in creation God's eternal power and Godhead, Rom. 1:20, we can see no less clearly that creation is tainted with evil. The Divine work is recognizable, but damaged; matter decomposes, plants have their diseases and die, animals devour each other. As for man, we recognize the truth expressed by the Apostle Paul: "..God gave them over to a reprobate mind, to do those things which are not convenient; being filled with all unrighteousness, fornication, wickedness, covetousness, maliciousness; full of envy, murder, debate, deceit, malignity; whisperers, backbiters, haters of God, despiteful, proud, boasters, inventors of evil things, disobedient to parents, without understanding, covenant breakers, without natural affection, implacable, unmerciful...," Rom. 1:28-31. Clearly, freedom and the other Divine gifts have been misused. The creature did not draw closer but rather wandered away from the source of Life and Freedom. What then has been happening?

That is stating the whole problem of evil: how could a perfect God create a world where sin is reigning? To resolve this problem some tried to avoid the contradiction between God and evil, either by assuming that God is not absolute, or, in effect, by denying the existence of evil. But if one reckons with the real freedom of the creature, one can retain the ideas of an absolute God and also of evil.[12]

It has been suggested by some that God Himself introduced evil into creation. But this is nonsense because evil is, by definition, that which is contrary to God's will. All that God does is necessarily good. The solution lies elsewhere. In a certain sense, evil is a lack of something, it is not something positive, created, willed. Evil is a lack of love, a deviation, a deficiency. To do evil is to not use that which God has made available; it is to take as center and goal, not the God Who IS, but the creature. On the other hand, evil can be a positive thing, when the creature makes a wrong use of what is good in itself, that is to say, when the creature diverts the Divine gifts from their true purpose and consciously acts against Divine will.

Let us very briefly examine what Scripture tells us about original creation. We must therefore attempt an exegesis of the first verses of Genesis. However, the extremely abundant literature on this subject [13] shows that these texts can be interpreted in various ways. Retaining the basic idea of the full inspiration of the Scriptures, we will choose those which are in the closest agreement with other indications in the Bible, and are not in contradiction with the *facts* of observation. We will also take into account the following notes:

1. The Hebrew verb translated "to create" is never used of a human action. It designates a Divine intervention, which may also be exercised after the original creation, to produce beings which could not be produced by the immanent power already present in what will exist eventually. One can accept a "creative" evolution, but not a "natural" or "mechanical" evolution.

2. There does not exist in Hebrew a special term to express the notion of a "universe." Expressions such as "heaven and earth" are used to signify the totality of that which exists. However, "heaven and earth" may also, after original creation, refer to *a part* of that universe; for example, the earth and the atmospheric heaven, the sky.

3. The first verses do not explicitly speak of the creation of spiritual beings; these are included in the universe expressed by "heaven and earth."

4. Gen. 1:2: "And the earth was without form, and void; and darkness was upon the face of the deep" gives the impression of chaos. However, God does not create chaos for His work is perfect, Deut. 32:4. This chaos must be the result of a universal catastrophy, which is probably indicated by the Greek work "katabole" used several times in the NT to indicate a landmark of major importance in the history of the world.[14]

Taking the above comments into account, we believe that the best interpretation of the first verses of the Bible is as follows:

A. At some completely indeterminate period, there was a creation of a primitive universe worthy of God which included a part of the multitude of spiritual beings mentioned in other parts of the Bible. The mode of existence of this original cosmos escapes us completely. Such a creation was unknown to heathenism, which admitted the existence of formless primitive matter or of an original chaos.

B. There had been a fall of certain of these powerful spiritual beings, as we will see later. This must have brought about the partial destruction of this first cosmos at some undetermined date. From this may have resulted the chaotic, material universe which is being investigated by our astronomers. Some stars seem to have existed for millions of millions of years. The earth appears to have been formed about 5,000 million years ago. Gen. 1:2 may refer either to the liquid state of this earth (for the word "water" may indicate any kind of liquid), or to a more recent state when the earth was covered, at least for the greater part, by water, and when it was engulfed by heavy clouds which could not be penetrated by the rays of the sun. This would have happened on the fourth day. The idea of such a universal "destruction" has already been suggested by Origen (*De Princ. III, 5, 4*).

C. Then come the six "days" of Gen. 1:3-31 where God intervenes because the still-immanent powers surviving among the debris of primitive creation could not produce life, sensation, or spirit. A certain "evolution" may have taken place, but directed by God and therefore of a creative kind. We will return to this in the next chapter.

Let us now examine what the Word of God teaches us about these spiritual creatures and the fall of some of them.

Job 38:7 speaks of the "sons of God" (literally "sons of Elohim") who were present at the foundations of the earth. (The word Elohim indicates God as Creator.) The word Jehovah presents Him as Mediator, establishing covenants. Deut. 14:1 speaks of "children of Jehovah" but these are men. (See note 16 of Chapter III). This expression also appears in other texts[15], which clearly indicate that there are spiritual beings whose habitual sphere is "the heaven." These beings are often called "saints".[16] Since they "...never marry, nor are given in marriage..." (Matt. 22:30) they were initially created in considerable numbers, as Daniel 7:10 describes: "...thousand thousands ministered unto Him, and ten thousand times ten thousand stood before Him." John confirms that there were "myriads of myriads" of them (Rev. 5:11). Hebrews 12:22 speaks of "an innumerable company of angels," while Luke 2:13 mentions" a multitude of the heavenly host." The Old Testament frequently mentions this heavenly host. Then there are "powers, mights, and dominions" (Eph. 1:21), "cherubim"[17] and "seraphim" (Isa 6:2,6). Two of these spirits are called by their names: the Archangel Michael[18] and Gabriel (Dan. 9:21).

When we study the Scriptures, we discover that some of these spiritual beings are in the service of God, and others are in a state of rebellion. Here too, we get an idea of how the creature has made use of its freedom. And some specific details may be useful to refine our ideas. Ezekiel 28 speaks of "the prince of Tyrus," but the context far exceeds that "man," and aims at a spiritual being called, in verse 12, "king of Tyrus," of whom the man was merely an earthly type. In this verse, we read:

> "Thou sealest up the sum, full of wisdom, and perfect in beauty.[19] Thou hast been in Eden the garden of God,[20] every precious stone was thy covering... Thou was the anointed cherub that covereth; and I have set thee so: thou wast upon the holy mountain of God; thou has walked up and down in the midst of the stones of fire. Thou wast perfect in thy ways from the day that thou wast created, till iniquity was found in thee. By the multitude of thy merchandise they have filled the midst of thee with violence, and thou has sinned: therefore, I will cast thee as profane out of the mountain of God: and I will destroy thee, O covering cherub, from the midst of the stones of fire. Thine heart was lifted up because of thy beauty..."[21]

Isaiah 14:12-15 also gives us a description which it would be difficult not to apply to the same being: "How art thou fallen from heaven, O Lucifer, son of the morning! How art thou cut down to the ground, which didst weaken the nations! For thou hast said in thine heart, I will sit also upon the mount of the congregation, in the sides of the north: I will ascend above the heights of the clouds; I will be like the Most High. Yet thou shalt be brought down to hell, to the sides of the pit."

So here we see a being placed in a very high position, created upright, but who became filled with pride. He not only turned away from God and took himself as center, but he wanted to become equal to God. Having rejected the Truth, he became the Lie. John says of the devil that there is no truth in him, that he is the father of the lie (John 8:44), that he sinned from the beginning[22]. That he was not alone in his rebellion is clear from the texts which speak of wrestling "against principalities, powers, rulers of the darkness of this world, spiritual wickedness in high places" (Eph. 6:12). These evil spirits are often spoken of, and in the future will make a final attempt (Rev. 12:7, 13 etc.) at setting up a kingdom of darkness. We can thus understand that a purification of certain heavenly things is necessary (Heb. 9:23). Later on we will see the misdeeds caused on earth by those fallen angels, and their continual opposition to the purposes of God.[23]

In summary, primitive creature has not made good use of the Divine gifts, and the consequences of this failure had to be enormous. It is not easy to elevate ourselves out of our small world up to the problems of the kind we are examining; we tend only too readily to reduce everything down to the level of our limited human views. God's magnificent creature turned away and opposed itself to Him Who is Love, Light, Unity, Truth, Logic, Life. The result had to be hate darkness, chaos, lies, confusion, death.

We might well ask ourselves what would have happened in the case where the creature would have firmed up its freedom by uniting itself voluntarily to its Creator. The age which has ended in the destruction of at least part of creation would have led to the state where God would have been "all in all." We would then have had the situation depicted as follows:

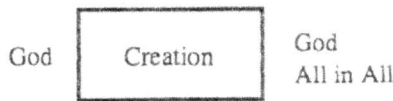

God	Creation	God All in All

But, because of primitive fall, it is the following sketch which represents the sequence of events:

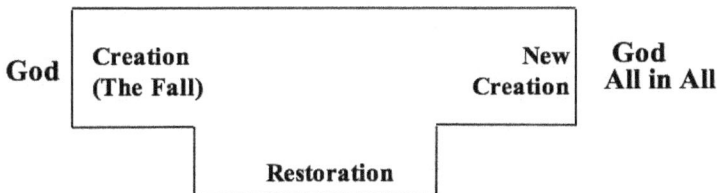

God	Creation (The Fall)	New Creation	God All in All
	Restoration		

In the following chapters we will attempt to examine how God acts to restore creation.

Note also that the fall of this creation is not a necessity, caused by its lack of perfection, but that it was brought to the fall through the wrong use of that which is perfectible. The imperfect creature is not *necessarily* sinful, since it is *free*. It becomes sinful when it resists God, wrongly uses its faculties, and sets up its own will against that of God. The creature is fully responsible.

The advent of sin brings destruction and requires restoration. All this period of restoration still belongs in the sphere of sin, and the creature cannot elevate itself up to God by its own efforts.

One becomes aware of the consequences of sin: a conflict has been created between the Justice and the Love of God. By His Justice He must necessarily condemn – God cannot arrange that by turning away from Him one is drawn closer to Him. He cannot let His creature become "a god" in His place. It must necessarily be that all that attacks the Unity will lead to chaos and death. But, nevertheless, God created through love for the creature; He wills that the creature "be" and it must reach its goal freely. After the fall, not only is there a lack of glory to be replenished, but first the creature, which separated itself from God, must return to Him. Love and Justice must therefore subsist integrally and be fully satisfied. Humanly, it is impossible to find a solution to this conflict – but what is impossible for us is not impossible for God.

THE ANCIENT WORLD

Only the Word of God can teach us how the Creator became Renovator. The world was reduced to a chaotic state by sin, the first age ended in disaster. Through love, God is going to, not repair, but reconstruct; not improve, but prepare a new age.[24] Gen. 1:3-31 gives us a glimpse, brief and masterly, of the acts of God: the six "days" of the reconstruction of the earth.

A thorough examination shows that those six "days" relate to the major geological periods. Indeed, there exists a remarkable agreement between the *characteristic features* of those ancient times, known of geology, and the sketchy data given in Scriptures. Since the Bible thus provides us with exact indications about things known only recently through man's efforts, we have here a "practical" proof of the inspiration of the Bible.

Modern scientific methods, and particularly the application of radioactive phenomena, enable us to determine the order of magnitude of the periods during which those events were taking place. Taking the four last "days" as a whole, one must allow for a period of some 500 million years.[25]

The original text uses the verb "to create" solely for animals of the sea and humanity. During the second "day," God created the expanse which we call "atmosphere." We may note that the work of the second "day" is not called "good," as is the case for the other "days." One might surmise that this is due to the presence of those spiritual beings whose fall caused the chaos. At the creation of humanity, Gen. 1, no details are given as to the time or the place where it happened. This humanity may include all the beings who lived several hundred thousand years ago and who did not yet have the structure or the culture of modern man. And at the beginning of Chapter II we are told that there was not then any man *to cultivate the soil*. It is only later that the creation of Adam took place, in a well-defined area (Mesopotamia), at a clearly indicated period (some 4000 to 5000 years before Jesus Christ according to the genealogy given in Gen. 5), and who was the father of humanity proper cultivating the soil and farming cattle.[26]

Archeology confirms that modern man originated at this location and at that time (end of the Neolithic era), and is characterized by the systematic cultivation of the soil and the breeding of cattle. Here again we find a remarkable scientific confirmation of the exactitude of the inspired text.

God formed man "out of the dust of the earth," which indicates his earthly origin, in contrast with the "second man" who is from heaven (1 Cor. 15:47). Man is not only created a "living soul," as are the animals, but in the Image of God. Now several texts tell us that Christ is the Image of God,[27] He created man in His likeness. Apart from an outward likeness, man also possesses conscience, intelligence, reason, will, freedom. Eccl. 7:29 teaches us that man was created upright. Therefore, there was not any germ of sin in him; he did not, however, possess immortality: to maintain life he needed "the tree of life" (Gen. 3:22). The moment this tree became inaccessible, Adam began to die.[28] Only God is immortal (1 Tim. 6:16) and unalterable,[29] and thus differs from all the creatures, who possess only a small reserve of life within themselves,[30] and thus always remain dependent upon the source of Life: God as Mediator.

The seventh "day" God *ceased* to create, which does not mean that He rested, as if He were tired.[31]

Let us now research what the mission was which God entrusted to Adam. According to several texts,[32] there was mentioned, since the "foundation" of the world, a "kingdom" on earth. Now we learn that Adam was to have dominion over the sea, the air (atmosphere), and the earth (Gen. 1:26-28). Psalm 8 goes further: "What is man, that Thou art mindful of him? And the son of man, that Thou visitest him? For Thou hast made him a little lower than the angels (see also Heb. 2:7), and hast crowned him with glory and honour. Thou madest him to have dominion over the works of Thy hands; Thou hast put all things under his feet: All sheep and oxen, yea, and the beasts of the field; the fowl of the air, and the fish of the sea, and whatsoever passeth through the paths of the sea."

Thus, Adam was to dominate the earth, to be king. God wants to use a creature for the overall restoration of the earth. But before he would be able to perform his mission, Adam had "to make firm his vocation and his election." He was to achieve this through a good use of the faculties which God had given Him for this purpose. Evil, that is to say that which is contrary to the will of God was to be alien to him. In all things he had to depend upon God and not choose an autonomous position by wanting to decide for himself what he judged to be good or bad.

Here also we face the difficulty of visualizing Adam's situation in his state of justice, which differs completely from our present (fallen) state. He had our faculties, but developed to the maximum, and not subject to the senses and matter. A knowledge which to us would be "supra-normal" enabled him, among other things, to give each animal a name which corresponded to its essential being. He heard God directly through his spirit. And so he carried a far heavier responsibility than we do, and disobedience on his part had to result in catastrophic consequences for him and for creation.

Scripture tells us that Adam, nevertheless, allowed himself to deviate from God's will and took an autonomous position. Instead of realizing himself fully, he lost himself by straying away from God. Let us take a look at the circumstances under which this happened. In order to avoid defective human interpretations as much as possible, it will be prudent to refer to the original text. The Authorized version reads, Gen. 3: "Now the serpent was more subtle than any beast of the field...". But the word translated "beast" indicates in general a living being, and the word translated "field" has the wider meaning of "country" or "territory".[33] This is about a living being which did not belong to the "garden of Eden" prepared for Adam. We turn to the Word for a definition of this living being called "serpent."

We receive a first indication by the structure of Gen. 3:1-24:

A	1-5 The "serpent"
B	6 The tree of knowledge
C	7 Effect produced on the man and woman. Human action: aprons
D	8-12 God's enquiry of the man
E	13 God's enquiry of the woman
F	14 Sentence passed on the "serpent"
E	16 Divine sentence on the woman
D	17-19 Divine sentence on the man
C	20 Effect produced on man and woman; v. 21: Divine action, coats of skin
B	22-24 The tree of life
A	24 Cherubim

We note the correlation between A and A, B and B etc. The cherubim of verse 24 are the counterpart of the "serpent" of verse 1. Because the cherubim are spirits, it seems that the being called "serpent" must also be spirit. The New Testament quite positively teaches us that there is question of, not only an animal, but of Satan, also called "serpent".[34] We have already seen (in Chapter II) that Satan was one of the cherubim, and so we find here a confirmation of what seemed logical to deduce from the above structure. Verse 15: "…I will put enmity between thee and the woman, and between thy seed and her Seed; it shall bruise thy head, and thou shalt bruise His heel" clearly shows that the subject in question is indeed Satan and not an animal (or a "beast").

We can also better understand what happened by referring to the words of the Apostle Paul. After talking about Eve being deceived, he says that Satan disguises himself as an angel of light (2 Cor. 11:3, 14). We are therefore well justified in believing that Satan, the fallen cherub who opposed God and wanted to prevent the realization of the Kingdom by Adam, presented himself to Eve as an angel of light. He questioned that which God had asserted, and imputed false motives to the Divine ordinances. Eve, greatly impressed by this dazzling apparition, allowed herself to be seduced and to act against the will of God. Adam associated himself with this attitude and carried its full responsibility: this is the spiritual separation from God, the fall. [35]Adam, fully conscious of the seriousness of the resulting consequences, used his own judgment as norm, thus disregarding God as God. Having fallen from his state of justice, he lost his spiritual faculties which distinguished him from us and which had enabled him to know God and creation directly through his spirit. He was thus reduced to our present state, subject to matter and the senses. So he missed the goal for which God had placed him in the garden of Eden: he sinned. Having the possibility to will that which is good, i.e., that which conforms to God's will, he chose his own will. This sin could be fully imputed to him and its consequences could not fail to follow.

Thus once more, the creature has wrongly used the grace of God. Neither Adam nor Eve raised themselves against God, as Satan had done, but they nevertheless turned away from Him. Separation from God corresponds to spiritual death, and physically their life became limited.[36] They were deprived of the glory of God.[37] Instead of ruling over the earth, they had to fight animals and the elements. The earth itself was affected by the fall, the ground was cursed (Rom. 8:22). Adam's children will be in his own likeness (Gen. 5:3) – "a clean thing does not come out of an unclean one" (Job. 14:4). Since then, therefore, all of Adam's posterity finds itself, by birth, in the same state: separated spiritually from God, devoid of glory, having their spirit darkened, subject, to corruption, dying, slave to sin. Men die, not because they sin personally but because they are sons of Adam. They are not punished for what Adam has done, but they suffer from the consequences of the state in which they are born.[38]

But all is not lost: God speaks of "the posterity of the woman." Through this Posterity the Divine plan will be realized, the Kingdom on earth established, but without struggle. Nevertheless, the love of God will be victorious, the Posterity will bruise the head of the "serpent."

Immediately Satan begins the fight: the "sons of Elohim," the fallen angels, appear on earth and corrupt it with their monstrous progeny.[39] Those evil spirits succeed in corrupting the whole earth (Gen. 6:5-12). Only Noah is an exception, having been found "just" and "perfect." In order to shield from corruption, the stock from whence the promised Posterity is to come, a general cleansing is necessary: it is the flood, which ends the second age. This age had begun under conditions corresponding to those of the Kingdom, but the fall of Adam prevented its immediate realization. Once more all seemed lost, but God prepared a new age, the one in which we now live. The previous sketch now becomes as shown below.

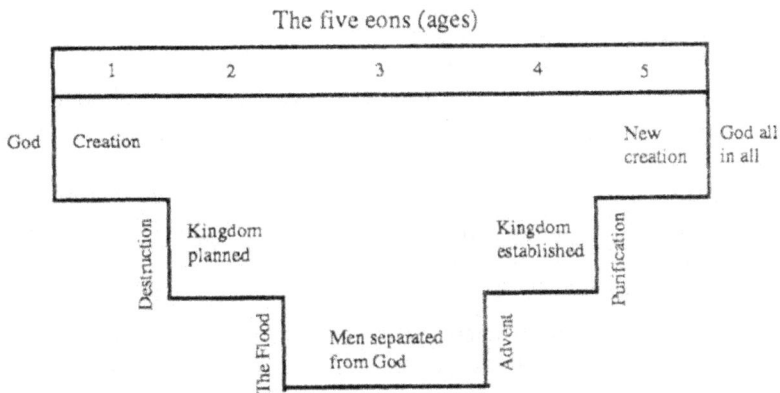

The five eons (ages)

Humanity is spiritually separated from God. In this evil age, God will show the greatness of His love to bring back humanity to Him. Following this, it will become possible to establish the Kingdom on earth, then creation will be renewed, leading to the final goal where God will be all in all. So we can identify five ages, or eons, through which creation must pass.

THE PRESENT EVIL AGE

a. The Abrahamic Covenants

After the flood the climate changes, at least in so far as the region where the Adamic race started is concerned. Before the flood, rain did not fall on that region;[40] thus rainbows could only appear after the flood. The rainbow recalls the covenant with Noah, his son, and all living creatures (Gen. 9:13, 16). As long as the earth remains in its present state, i.e. during the entire age in which we now live, "seedtime and harvest, and cold and heat, and summer and winter, and day and night shall not cease" (Gen. 8:22). It is probably due to these new circumstances that the length of life, which before the flood was habitually of several hundreds of years, rapidly decreased after a period of stabilization down to the current span of some 80 years, which today is considered to be quite an advanced age (Ps. 90:10).

We may note that during the fourth age, that of the Kingdom on earth, the span of normal life will be increased again, such that a hundred-year old man will still be considered "a child" (Isa. 65:20). Thus there is here a correlation between the second age – where the Kingdom virtually begins with Adam – and the fourth age where the Kingdom is established. Similarly, the fifth age, that of the New Creation, appears to correspond, as far as the environmental conditions are concerned, with the first age and original creation. (After the sixth day, God ceased to create; in the fifth age, as in the first, God creates again.)

God chose Noah, a righteous man, and delivers the earth and the sea to him.[41] Then the blessings pass on to Shem (Gen. 9:26). The 70 nations descended from the sons of Noah were to scatter over the earth. One group of Noachides, probably led by Nimrod, founded Babel (Gen. 10:8-10, 11:4) and built his tower, the ziggurat named "Etemenanka," i.e., "the house of the foundation of the heaven and the earth."[42] All had the same spirit of rebellion against Divine will by not wanting to disperse all over the earth. It is in this sense that they all had the same "*language*," the ability to communicate, but not the same *tongue*, the same pride which is spoken of in Luke 1:51. But this common, mutual feeling was confounded by the Lord. As a result of this confusion of feelings, they could no longer live together and so dispersed.[43]

God will not achieve His goal through the masses of men who, having recognized God in His works, have not glorified Him as God. They have given themselves up to uncleanness and evil (Rom. 1:18-32). God chooses individuals who will have special missions to perform for the benefit of others. Here we see the principle of election, which operates not for the blessing of the elected but more particularly for that of the non-elected through the elected. Following Adam, Noah and Seth, comes Abraham. In Gen. 12:1 the Lord said unto Abram: "Get thee out of thy country, and from thy kindred, and from thy father's house, unto a land that I will shew thee: And I will make of thee a great nation." When he had left not only his native land but also "the house of his father" (by separating himself from Lot), the land promised to him and his posterity (Gen. 12:7, 13:14, 15; 15:7, 18) was shown to him, Gen. 13:15-17. It extends from the river of Egypt to the river Euphrates (Gen. 15:18).[44] It is the land of Canaan, which he will possess during the age in which the promise will be realized, Gen. 17:8.[45] This implies the resurrection of Abraham.

It is clear that this is literally about a well-determined land and a *nation*, that is, a group of men living in one particular area and under one government. As the NT tells us, this promise has not yet been accomplished: "He gave him none inheritance in it," Acts 7:5; "By faith he sojourned in the land of promise, as in a strange country, dwelling in tabernacles with Isaac and Jacob, the heirs with him of the same promise," Heb. 11:9.

It is in relation to those earthly promises that it is said that all the families of the earth will be blessed, Gen. 12:2; Acts 3:25. The "everlasting" covenant, i.e., the covenant relating to the coming age that the Lord was thus establishing with Abraham was sealed by the sign of circumcision, Gen. 17:10, 14.

Let us note that these are unconditional promises, in the sense that their realization does not depend on the degree of faithfulness of Abraham or his posterity. Their accomplishment, since it depends only on God, is thus certain and total. But it is evident that any man who belongs to Abraham's posterity will partake of these promises only if he has life during the coming age, that is, if he has a part in the "eonian" life on earth.

All this concerns the earth and not "heaven," a *nation* and not a spiritual group. But, reckoning with the teachings of the Apostle Paul, it is clear that Abraham also has a "heavenly" posterity, in relation to which there is no question of men circumcised in the flesh, of a country, of a nation; rather, it is about the uncircumcision (Rom. 3:30; 4:9-12), about possession of the world (Rom. 4:13), about Abraham being made the father of many nations (Rom. 4:17, 18; Gal. 3:8).

Here it is about heavenly blessings, not earthly ones, and it is in relation to this spiritual heavenly position that the Apostle to the gentiles speaks of justification by faith, based on the faith of Abraham mentioned in Gen. 15:1-6 which preceded circumcision, Rom. 4:9-12.

Now, we see in Gen. 12:3 and 17:5 that already it was said Abraham would be the father of many nations (therefore of a multitude of people making up these nations) and that all the nations will be blessed in Abraham. The OT thus is really referring to two clearly distinct posterities: on one hand a great *nation* made up of men circumcised in the flesh and who will possess the land of Canaan, and on the other hand, a group of men out of all the nations, who are justified by faith as was Abraham.

The blessings promised to Abraham will apply, on one hand, to all the families of the earth *through the medium of the nation* descended from Abraham, but, on the other hand, also *directly* ("in thee," Gen. 12:3; 17:5) to the people of all the nations. It is understood that this distinction is not yet clearly expressed in the OT; the revelations granted only to Paul were needed to explain more precisely these promises.[46]

The earthly promises concerning a nation and a country passed on to Isaac, Gen. 21:22, to Jacob, Gen. 28:3, 4 and to Judah, Gen. 49:10.[47]

When Isaac and Jacob (Israel) are mentioned together with Abraham, it is the earthly promises and the nation of Israel that are in view. This applies equally to the NT, for example in Matt. 8:11 and Luke 13:28 where "the Kingdom of God" refers to a Kingdom of heavenly *origin*, but established on earth, as we will see later on.

We may note Satan's repeated attacks against the posterity: when Abraham lingered in Haran (Gen. 11:31) rather than obeying the Lord immediately, the Canaanite occupied the promised land (Gen. 12:6); and these belonged to the accursed race of the "sons of Elohim"[48] who were to be destroyed by Israel.

Among other attacks, we have: the famine which drives Israel to Egypt, the massacre of the male children of Israel (Ex. 1:16), oppression in Egypt, the pursuit to the Red Sea (Ex. 14:8). We will meet other examples later.

Let us note, in passing, the Passover at the exodus from Egypt. This was a symbol of the future deliverance of Israel and of its return to the land when the true Lamb would be sacrificed. Just as, in Egypt, Israelites had to cover themselves with the blood of the lamb to be delivered from death, so they will have to come into communion with the Lord and be covered by His Sacrifice in order to partake of the eonian life on earth.

b. The Law and the Old Covenant

Up to this time sin was in the world, but sin was not imputed to men, Rom. 5:13, because they did not fully understand their state as sinners. Personally, they were not (or little) responsible. In order to freely leave this state of sin and of estrangement from God, they needed to become conscious of the state in which they found themselves by birth. Thus they had to learn that sin is the transgression of the Law (1 John 3:4), above all to know this Law, what God wanted from them, to know what was good and profitable.

Logically, the man who believes in God who understands what He wants, should realize that he is by nature incapable to accomplish this: he recognizes his state of sin. He should then turn to his Creator to be helped by Him.

But "natural man" is not very reasonable, precisely because he is in a state of sin. Experience demonstrates that, at all times, man, placed in front of Divine Will, assumes faulty attitudes; he may, in his vanity, pretend to be capable to act according to this Will, or he feels that God is asking too much, or he remains indifferent, or he may even deny the very existence of God.

God having created, from the progeny of Abraham, Isaac, and Jacob, a people to serve as instrument for the restoration of humanity, this people had first of all to be persuaded of their sinful condition and appeal to Divine grace. They had therefore to be instructed by God. We know that this people received, through Moses and the angels (Deut. 33:2; Acts

7:53; Gal. 3:19), a Law, that is, a set of instructions and ordinances applying specifically to them.

This Law may be subdivided as follows:

1. The commandments addressed to Israel, Ex. 20:1-26.
2. The laws for the social life of Israel, Ex. 21:1 to 24:11.
3. The ceremonies of Israel, Ex. 24:12 to 31:18.

Taken together, these constitute "the Law, given exclusively to the chosen people – although the basis for the Law and many "commandments" therein are obviously also applicable to all men – and can be completely observed only in their land and while the Temple is in existence.

This Law is far from being rudimentary and from being concerned merely with external things. Not only does it give the "ten commandments," which are of major importance, but it indicates the foundation upon which it rests: "Thou shalt love the Lord thy God with all thine heart, and with all thy soul, and with all thy might." (Deut. 6:5; 10:12, 13. "Thou shalt love thy neighbor as thyself." Lev. 19:18.[49]

Our Lord has confirmed that this is the first and great commandment and that the second is like unto it, and that on these two commandments hang all the Law and the Prophets.[50] The laws for the social life and for the ceremonies of Israel were nothing without this foundation; the prophets have insisted on this point.[51] The OT required not only for circumcision of the flesh, as a sign of the Covenant with Israel, but especially that of the heart (Deut. 10:16, Jer. 4:9; 9:25, 26). Israel was to "fear" the Lord, walk in His ways, love and serve the Lord with all their heart and soul, Deut. 10:12-16.

The offerings concerned the consciousness of sin, confession of sin, the search for a good relationship with God, the giving up of self unto God, the gratitude for blessings received, etc. These offerings were not for those who opposed themselves deliberately against God, who acted "presumptuously," for these were to be cut-off from among His people, Num. 15:30.

The sacrifices for sin, Lev. 4:3, for trespass, Lev. 5:7, the offerings, Lev. 14:20, all related to the idea that sin could be "covered" by the spiritual reality represented by these ceremonies, the sacrifice of the Divine Lamb.[52]

The feasts summarized the main events in the history of the chosen people. The feast of the "atonement" was of major importance. While the offerings for sin and for trespasses enabled the individual sinner – by the fact that his sin was "covered" – to retain membership in the community of Israel (the other offerings also concerning the individual), the main goal of the feast of "atonement," which included the rite described in Lev. 16 where blood was sprinkled on the arc of the covenant in the Holy of Holies, was to maintain the covenant with the elected people in spite of the sins of this people taken as a whole.

One can thus well understand that all those ceremonies had no value in themselves and that God did not require them for Himself, but that they had been instituted in order to help a people who were not yet sufficiently developed so they could directly understand abstract notions and who therefore needed visible representations of invisible realities.

Thus was Israel educated by the Law and acquainted with the will of God, Rom. 2:18. This people should should have closed their mouth and realized that they were guilty before God, Rom. 3:19, because it is the Law that gives the knowledge of sin, Rom. 3:20, and causes sin to abound (Rom. 5:20; 7:13; Gal. 3:19).

But what did Israel do? Even before they learned what was asked of them, the entire people declared: "All that the Lord hath spoken we will do," Ex. 19:8. And they repeat this after they had heard the commandments and the laws, Ex. 24:1-3, 7, 8.

The fundamental error committed by the majority of the sons of Israel thus was that they believed that they could observe the Law by their own efforts and be justified by the works of the Law. It is true that Moses had said: "The man which doeth those things shall live by them," Rom. 10:5; but the question was: "How could they put them into practice?" The Law told them what they had to do, but did not provide natural man, in bondage to sin, the power to accomplish it.

It is this state of sin that they should have recognized, as well as the necessity of Divine grace. Numerous texts in the OT spoke of this. Thus Deut. 8:17, 18: "And thou say in thine heart, my power and the might of mine hand hath gotten me this wealth. But thou shalt remember the Lord thy God: for it is He that giveth thee power to acquire wealth…"

Because they did not resort to God's grace they became *slaves* of the Law, "in bondage under the elements of the world," Gal. 4:3, placing themselves *under* the Law,[53] under the curse, Gal. 3:10, 13, because they had said "Amen" upon the words: "Cursed be he that confirmeth not all the words of this law to do them," Deut. 27:26; Gal. 3:10.

It is very important to note that it is after this promise to do all that the Lord had said that Moses sprinkled the blood of bulls upon the people saying: "Behold the blood of the covenant, which the Lord hath made with you concerning all these words," Ex. 24:8.

This Sinai covenant relates to the covenants made with Abraham, but yet differs from them completely. When the Lord speaks of them to the sons of Israel in the land of Moab, He says: "That thou shouldest enter into covenant with the Lord their God, and into his oath, which the Lord their God maketh with thee this day: that he may be unto thee a God, as he hath said unto thee, and as he hath sworn unto thy fathers, to Abraham, to Isaac, and to Jacob," Deut. 29:12, 13. The Lord particularly warns them against idolatry, v. 18, against the inclinations of the natural heart, v. 19. Deut. 30 summarizes the blessings which would follow an obedience to all that is prescribed; they were to love the Lord, walk in His ways, and keep His commandments, His statutes and His judgments that they might live, Deut. 30:16.

The characteristic of this covenant thus is that the man who puts the laws and statutes into practice will live by them, Lev. 18:5. According to the Apostle Paul, that is how Moses defines the righteousness which is of the law, Rom. 10:5. But to put all this into practice, it needed that God first gave them a heart to understand, eyes to see, and ears to hear; these gracious gifts had not yet been received by them when they entered the land of Moab, Deut. 29:4.

So we can see that this Sinai covenant is completely distinct from those covenants made with Abraham, Phineas, David, Isaac, and Jacob which were unconditional, since all hinges on the future behavior of Israel.

Further, it is said of the first covenants that they are "eternal," i.e., that they would last during the entire age to come; this has never been said of the Sinai covenant. To the contrary, this old covenant will be replaced by a new covenant, as we will see below.

On the other hand, one must carefully distinguish between the Law and the Sinai covenant. The Law reveals what the Lord desires from His people, without giving the means to accomplish it. The covenant required that the Law be observed totally, but the sons of Israel understood it in the sense that they could by themselves do all that the Lord had asked, without change of heart, i.e. without Divine intervention in their heart.

This distinction between the Law and the Old Covenant is, besides, characterized by the fact that the Law remains in force during the age to come, while the Old Covenant will be replaced by a New Covenant. Let us examine these two points.

Numerous texts[54] indicate that the Law is "everlasting" i.e. that it is still in force during the "olam" (age) to come, just as the covenants with Abraham and his earthly posterity are said to be "everlasting."

As long as the people of Israel remain the people of God and reside in their land, the Law is applicable. We will see below that the Lord himself has confirmed this when He said: "For verily I say unto you till heaven and earth pass, one jot or one tittle shall in no wise pass from the law, till all be fulfilled." Matt. 5:18. Now, the heaven and the earth will not "pass" until the end of the next age, when "a new heaven and a new earth" will come, Rev. 21:1; 2 Pet. 3:10. Israel will then have accomplished their mission and will cease to exist as an earthly nation. We will see that in the new creation there will be neither Jew or Gentile.

Ezekiel chapters 40 to 45 give us a detailed description of the Temple and the ceremonies of the age to come. Note in passing that the circumcision of the flesh, a sign, of the "everlasting" covenant with Abraham and his earthly posterity, Gen. 17:7, and the animal offerings are mentioned there. (See Eze. 44:9 for the circumcision of the flesh.)

But if the Law – though somewhat modified because of what has been accomplished since – remains in force, the Old Covenant will be replaced by a New Covenant which will enable the people to observe all the Law.[55] It is mainly the prophet Jeremiah who speaks of this New Covenant: "Behold, the days come, saith the Lord, that I will make a new covenant with the house of Israel, and with the house of Judah: not according to the covenant that I made with their fathers in the day that I took them by the hand to bring them out of the land of Egypt; which My covenant they brake...", Jer. 31:31, 32. Note well that this New covenant concerns the house of Israel and the house of Judah, the same *nation* with whom the Sinai covenant was made. And Jeremiah adds: "But this shall be the covenant that I will make with the house of Israel; after those days, saith the Lord, I will put My law in their inward parts, and write it in their hearts; and will be their God, and they shall be My people." These words are recalled in Heb. 8:8-12 and 10:16, 17, an Epistle addressed to Christian Jews.

Eze. 36 also speaks of this new heart and spirit when they will live in *the land given to their fathers*. This will be the realization of that which was announced in Deut. 30:6: "And the Lord thy God will circumcise thine heart, and the heart of thy seed, to love the Lord thy God with all thine heart, and with all thy soul, that thou mayest live." It is after this conversion that they will be able to practice all the commandments prescribed through the intermediary of Moses, v. 8. Eze. 11:19, 20 also says: "And I will give them one heart, and I will put a new spirit within you; and I will take the stony heart out of their flesh, and will give them a heart of flesh: *"that they may walk in* My statutes, and keep Mine ordinances, and do them."

Here, too, the Word tells us that the Law will not be abolished, but will be accomplished through Divine grace. The essential difference between the Old and the New Covenants thus lies in *the manner* in which the Law is observed: either through human effort, in order to be justified by the works of the Law, or as a result of a spiritual action from God on man who then realizes his state of sin and turns to Him – not as "work" but through love.

This New Covenant will be the outcome of the "everlasting" Abrahamic covenants. It will, in fact, be a Covenant of "everlasting" peace (Isa. 55:3; 61:8; Jer. 32:40; Eze. 16:30; 34:25; 37:26), and the sanctuary, i.e. the Temple, will be in the midst of them during the entire age to come, Eze. 37:26 and Chapters 41 to 47.

We will return to this New Covenant when we examine the NT. Let us also note that after speaking of the New Covenant, Jeremiah adds: "If those ordinances (statutes relating to the laws of nature) depart from before Me, saith the Lord, then the seed of Israel also shall cease from being a nation before Me for ever. Thus saith the Lord; if heaven above can be measured, and the foundations of the earth searched out beneath, I will also cast off all the seed of Israel for all that they have done, saith the Lord.", Jer. 31:36, 37. Note the insistence on the fact that these are indeed the words of the Lord. One could hardly express more clearly and positively than is done in this entire chapter the *national* and religious restoration of the people of Israel, of this *nation* in the *land* promised to their fathers.

The first five books of the Bible, which, as an ensemble are called "the Law",[56] contain many prophecies concerning Israel's future, the dispersion, the return, and the accomplishment of the earthly Abrahamic promises. We cite only a few texts:

> "And the Lord shall scatter thee among all people, from the one end of the earth even unto the other; and there thou shalt serve other gods, which neither thou nor thy fathers have known, even wood and stone. And among these nations shalt thou find no ease, neither shall the sole of thy foot have rest: but the Lord shall give thee there a trembling heart, and failing of eyes, and sorrow of mind: And thy life shall hang in doubt before thee; and thou shall fear day and night, and shall have none assurance of thy life…", Deut. 28:64-66.

> "…when all these things are come upon thee, the blessing and the curse, which I have set upon thee, and thou shalt call them to mind among all the nations, whither the Lord thy God hath driven thee, And shalt return to the Lord thy God, and shalt obey his voice according to all that I command thee this day, thou and thy children, with all thine heart, and with all thy soul; That then the Lord thy God will turn thy captivity, and have compassion upon thee, and will return and gather thee from all the nations, whither the Lord thy God hath scattered thee. If any of thine be driven out unto the outmost parts of heaven, from thence will the Lord thy God gather thee, and from thence will He fetch thee: And the Lord thy God will bring thee into the land which thy fathers possessed, and thou shalt possess it; and He will do thee good, and multiply thee above thy fathers. Deut. 30:1-5.

> "And ye shall perish among the heathen, and the land of your enemies shall eat you up. And they that are left of you shall pine

away in their iniquity in your enemies' lands; and also in the iniquities of their fathers shall they pine away with them. If they shall confess their iniquity, and the iniquity of their fathers, with their trespass which they trespassed against Me, and that also they have walked contrary unto Me; And that I also have walked contrary unto them, and have brought them into the land of their enemies; if then their uncircumcised hearts be humbled, and they then accept the punishment of their iniquity; Then will I remember my covenant with Jacob, and also my covenant with Isaac, and also my covenant with Abraham will I remember; and I will remember the land. The land also shall be left of them, and shall enjoy her Sabbaths, while she lieth desolate without them: and they shall accept of the punishment of their iniquity; because, even because they despised my judgments, and because their soul abhorred my statutes. And yet for all that, when they be in the land of their enemies, I will not cast them away, neither will I abhor them, to destroy them utterly, and to break my covenant with them: for I am the Lord their God. But I will for their sakes remember the covenant of their ancestors, whom I brought forth out of the land of Egypt in the sight of the heathen, that I might be their God: I am the Lord." Lev. 26:38-45.

After their exodus from Egypt, the return to the promised land is delayed nearly 40 years because of their lack of faith, and when the people enter it; there they find the posterity of Satan, which they must destroy. They do not do this completely and suffer the harsh consequences of their disobedience.[57]

The restoration and the Kingdom are continually held up before the Israelites' eyes. When they ask Samuel to give them a king, as the other peoples have, the Lord says: "...they have rejected me, that I should not reign over them." 1 Sam. 8:7.

David represents the earthly type of King. His struggles against Satan's posterity are well known.[58] He establishes himself in Jerusalem, thereby marking one more step toward the realization of the Kingdom on earth. For we now have the posterity, the land the king, and the city. But the true King is yet to come: "...I will set up thy seed after thee, which shall proceed out of thy bowels, and I will establish His kingdom.", 2 Sam. 7:12.

With Solomon the Kingdom seems to be very near. But the idols are still there, and Israel is again warned that they will be cut off out of the land and cast out if they turn away from God to serve Satan, 1 Kings 9:6, 7. Even Solomon allows himself to be carried away by the Canaanite women, corrupted by the cursed race issued from "the sons of Elohim."

Then follows the dismal history of the numerous kings, the division into 10 tribes and two tribes, and idolatry. One sees also the continuing efforts of Satan to prevent the coming of the posterity who will crush his head.[59] The call to repentance is still being heard, 2 Kings 17:13. But, finally, the momentous judgment is pronounced: "…Go and tell this people, hear ye indeed, but understand not; and see ye indeed, but perceive not. Make the heart of this people fat, and make their ears heavy, and shut their eyes; lest they see with their eyes, and hear with their ears, and understand with their heart, and convert, and be healed.", Isa. 6:9, 10.

Part of the people is led away into Assyria, then another part to Babylon. Jerusalem and the Temple are destroyed. The Kingdom seems so remote: "I will overturn, overturn, overturn it." But this is not final: "and it shall be no more until He come whose right it is; and I will give it to Him.", Eze. 21:27. Thus, here we see another, new, unconditional promise: it is the Posterity, pre-eminently, who will bring the Kingdom on earth.

Israel is now "Lo-Ammi," i.e. "not my people," Hosea 1:9.[60]

With Ezra and Nehemiah hope returns: the City and the Temple are rebuilt, the Word of God rediscovered. But one notes the immediate reaction of Satan, Ezra 4; 9:1; Neh. 4:7; 13:24. Zerubbabel and Joshua will not be kings, the people will have to wait for Him whose name is "The Branch": "Even He shall build the temple of the Lord; and He shall bear the glory, and shall sit and rule upon His throne; and He shall be a priest upon His throne; and the counsel of peace shall be between them both," Zech. 6:13.

This "Branch" is mentioned several times and is presented under four viewpoints corresponding to the four Gospels:

KING	SERVANT	MAN	GOD
I will raise Unto David a	I will bring Forth My Servant the	Behold the Man Whose Name is the	The BRANCH Of the Lord. Isa. 4:2

Righteous BRANCH, a King shall reign. Jer. 23:5, 6 Thy King cometh Zech. 9:9.	BRANCH. Zech. 3:8. Behold My Servant. Isa. 42:1.	BRANCH Zech. 6:12.	Behold your God. Isa. 40:9.
Matthew	Mark	Luke	John

c. The Witness of the Prophets

Before going further into a study of how God realizes His plan, we believe it would be useful to show how the prophets insist on the national and religious restoration of the elect People. They emphasize a spiritual attitude, but do not set aside the Law with all its commandments.

ISAIAH

2:2	The nations will flock to Jerusalem.
9:5, 6	The Son sits on the throne of David.
11:1-10	Situation changed during the Messianic reign.
11:11-16	Return of Israel, "…again, the second time…". (see Isa. 49)
14:1-3	Restoration of Israel.
29:18, 19	Messianic blessings.
32:15-18	The spirit poured from on high is a sign that the Kingdom is near.
35:3-6	The miraculous healings are signs of the coming of the Kingdom.
44:3	"I will pour My spirit upon thy seed."
44:6	"The Lord the King of Israel, and His Redeemer…"
45:25	"In the Lord shall all the seed of Israel be justified…"
46:13	"…I will place salvation in Zion for Israel My glory."
51:4	The Law, a light of the people.

53:1-12	The Savior.
54:6-8	Israel, as a woman forsaken for a small moment, but gathered with great mercies and kindness.
60:21	Inheritance of the land "for ever."
61:1, 2	The day of vengeance was to follow the times of the Gospels; the Kingdom comes after this.
61:6	Converted Jews will be called "Priests of the Lord." See also Ex. 19:6, "ye shall be unto Me a kingdom of priests…" and Isa. 66:21 "priests" and "Levites."
62:1-3	Jerusalem.
65:17-25	The new conditions under the Kingdom. The new heavens and the new earth do not correspond with those of Rev. 21. The Companion Bible shows the following contrasts:

	Isa. 65	Rev. 21
Name	Jerusalem	New Jerusalem
Position	On a mountain	Coming from heaven
Privileges	v. 18-20	v. 4
Characteristics	Sinners, Temple	no sinners, no
State	buildings, plantations	perfect

About the new heavens and the new earth, see also Luke 21:33; Ps. 102:27; Isa. 6; 2 Pet. 3:7-10.

66:19	"…they shall declare My glory among the nations."
66:23	The sabbath.

JEREMIAH

3:17-19	Jerusalem, throne of the Lord. All the nations will gather there. Judah and Israel, back in the land, shall call the Lord "My Father."
16:15	…I will bring them again into their land that I gave unto their fathers." See also v. 16 which speaks of "fishers," i.e.: of those who will attempt to bring them back into their land, and of "hunters," i.e.:

those who hunt down the Jews. One might, in this context, reflect on Zionism and anti-Semitism.

23:3-8   "I will gather the remnant of My flock out of all countries whither I have driven them…" The Branch King. Judah and Israel. A parallel between the exodus from Egypt and the return of the "posterity of the house of Israel" out of all the nations. "Then shall dwell in their own land."

It is impossible not to take these texts literally. The Branch has never been King, nor has Justice reigned.

24:7   "And I will give them an heart to know Me, that I am the Lord; and they shall be My People, and I shall be their God: for they shall return unto Me with their whole heart."

30:3-11   "For, lo, the days come, saith the Lord that I will bring again the captivity of My People Israel and Judah, saith the Lord: and I will cause them to return to the land that I gave to their fathers, and they shall possess it." The king David. Can this be expressed more clearly?

31:31-34 The New Covenant with Israel and Judah, in contrast with the Old Covenant with the same people. The Law written in their hearts.

31:35-37 "If heaven above can e measured and the foundations of the earth searched out beneath, I will also cast off all the seed of Israel for all that they have done, saith the Lord."

32:40   "Everlasting" covenant.

50:4-6   The children of Israel an of Judah shall come together. "Perpetual" covenant. Lost sheep.

EZEKIEL

11:17-20 "I will even gather you from the people, and assemble you out of the countries where ye have been scattered, and I will give you the land of Israel." New spirit, new heart, "that they may walk in My statutes and keep Mine ordinances, and do them."

16:60-63	"I will remember My covenant with thee in the days of thy youth, and I will establish unto thee an "everlasting" covenant." Covenant established. Repentance of Israel. Forgiveness.
28:25	"When I shall have gathered the house of Israel from the people among whom they are scattered, and shall be sanctified in them in the sight of the heathen, then shall they dwell in their land that I have given to My servant Jacob."
33:11	Conversion.
34:12-24	Return in the land, on the mountains of Israel, of the sheep scattered among the nations.
36:24-28	"For I will take you from among the heathen, and gather you out of all countries, and will bring you into your own land. Then will I sprinkle clean water upon you, and ye shall be clean: from all your filthiness, and from all your idols, will I cleanse you. A new heart also will I give you, and a new spirit will I put within you: and I will take away the stony heart out of your flesh, and I will give you an heart of flesh. And I will put My Spirit within you, and cause you to walk in My statutes, and ye shall keep My judgments, and do them. And ye shall dwell in the land that I gave to your fathers; and ye shall be My People, and I will be your God."
37.	The vision of the dry bones: the restoration of Israel. "…these bones are the entire house of Israel…"; "I will bring you into the land of Israel;" "I shall put My spirit in you."
37:24-28	David is king. Israel shall "walk in My judgments and observe My statutes;" "they shall dwell in the land that I have given unto Jacob My servant, wherein your fathers have dwelt;" "for ever;" "everlasting covenant;" "the heathen shall know that I the Lord do sanctify Israel."
39:29	"I have poured out My spirit upon the house of Israel."
40-46	The Temple. Offerings. Priests. Sabbaths. Passover. Circumcision of the flesh and of the heart (44:9). Division of the land among the 12 tribes.

DANIEL

9:24-27	Seventy weeks are determined upon the People and the holy City.
12:1	Michael, the great prince and defender of the sons of Israel arises. A time of distress. Resurrection.

JOEL

2:11-32	The great and terrible day of the Lord. Tribulations. Call to repentance. Promises to Israel. The spirit poured out upon all flesh. Spiritual gifts.

AMOS

9:11-15	The house of David raised up. Blessings. "I will bring again the captivity of My People of Israel." "They shall no more be pulled up out of their land which I have given them." Clearly, this and many other prophecies have not yet been realized.

ZECHARIAH

He prophesized *after* Israel's captivity; thus his prophecies can in no way be applied to the return of the Jews from Babylon.

8:22, 23	Blessings of peoples and nations through Israel.
9:9, 10	The coming of the Lord, the King of Israel, in His humility.
11:16	Antichrist.
12:1-10	Tribulations. "And I will pour upon the house of David, and upon the inhabitants of Jerusalem, the spirit of grace and of supplications: and they shall look upon Me Whom they have pierced…"
14:4-5	The coming of the Lord in glory.
14:16	The peoples come to Jerusalem to worship.

All these prophecies have often been considered either as having been already accomplished, or as not to be accomplished because of Israel's lack of faithfulness, or as having to be interpreted in a "spiritual" sense and applying them to the "Church." None of these solutions are acceptable if one admits that all Scriptures are fully inspired by God.

Certain prophecies have had a beginning of realization, but it is clear that the greater part of that which they encompass has never been realized.

On the other hand, a "spiritual" interpretation can be accepted up to a point, but, at the same time a literal realization must be maintained. If Israel is a symbolic people, then their *entire* history, past and future, must be considered and not be cut in two and the end denied. Only too often, the story of the past is taken in a literal and spiritual sense, but the story of the future is taken in a spiritual sense only. Besides, it is quite arbitrary to attribute the blessings to "the Church" and the curses to Israel.

We must also point out that individual blessings of some Jews in the future, after they have come to believe in Jesus Christ, is not a realization of the prophecies. These speak of a literal land which extends from the Nile to the Euphrates, of Jerusalem, of a nation governed by a King, etc. When the Jews will believe that Jesus is the Christ, they will be Christians, but will nevertheless remain Jews, and form a *nation* separated from the other nations. From the point of view of the new birth, of salvation, however, there will be no distinction between Jewish and non-Jewish Christians; in this sense there will be only one "Church." On the earth, one must reckon with the earthly blessings promised to the earthly posterity of Abraham. The heavenly posterity will find itself in closer communion with, God, "in Christ," where there will be neither Jew nor Gentile. We will look into these questions in greater detail later. (Also in *The Teachings of the Apostle Paul* and *The Way of Salvation*).

In the prophecies we can already distinguish two advents of the Lord: one advent in humility (for example Isa. 53) and a second advent in glory, followed by the Kingdom on earth. The latter can only come after Israel's repentance. The first advent was necessary for the sacrifice for sin, Isa. 53:10.

The dismal record of humanity since Adam shows that fallen man does not turn to God, that he is "under" sin and incapable of doing what God desires. If God reveals what is good and what he should then do in order to be blessed, it is not so that he can accomplish it through his own efforts, but so that he can recognize his state of sin and the necessity to have recourse to Divine grace. The law must lead men – and in the first place the elected people – to Christ, by Whom grace comes.[61]

Christ having come, Israel's responsibility was increased. Not only were they instructed by the Law, but they had before them The One Who could forgive sins, cause them to be born again, and render them capable, by the power of the Spirit, to do what God asked them to do.

It is remarkable to note that the expectation of a Savior was fairly widespread throughout the world shortly before the beginning of our era. This may be explained by a knowledge of the OT prophecies, for instance those of Daniel concerning the 70 weeks of years; these were imparted through the dispersion among the nations. Confucius, the Siamese, Tacitus, Suetone, Virgil speak of this expectation of a Messiah.

d. The Gospels

In the Gospels, we see a beginning of the literal realization of the prophecies given to Israel.

To accomplish our objective, it will be sufficient to demonstrate the following propositions:

1. Jesus Christ is the "Posterity of the Woman".

He is the son of David, son of Abraham, Matt. 1:1. Satan wastes no time to attack and try to kill Him (murder of the children of Bethlehem), or at least to make Him yield to temptations, Matt. 4.

2. Jesus is the Christ, i.e. the Messiah Announced by the Prophet.

"Jesus, Who is called Christ," Matt. 1:16, 16:16; Luke 2:11, 26; John 1:45; 11:27. It is known that "Christ" means "the anointed One" and corresponds to the Hebrew "Messiah." The name "Jesus" characterizes Him while in His humiliation, and it is not surprising that the demons and those who denied Him and crucified Him choose to call Him so rather than Christ, Jesus Christ, or Christ Jesus.

His baptism in water – a ceremony well known of by Jews – was to reveal to Israel that He was the Messiah, Matt. 3:15-17; John 1:31-34. The anointing was accompanied by a water baptism, Ex. 29:4-7; Lev. 8:6, 12.

The miracles also were to make Him known as the Messiah, Matt. 8:16, 17; 9:1-8, 18-33; 11:2-5; 12:28; 14:33; John 5:36; 10:24, 25. See also Isa. 29:18; 35:4-6; 42:7; 53:3; 61:1-3.

The "sheep," that is to say, the Jews of good will, were to so recognize Him, but not the others, John 10:26, 27.

It is most important, to us also, to note that the miracles were not performed for the benefit of unbelievers. Scripture emphasizes this: "An evil and adulterous generation seeketh after a sign; and there shall no sign be given to it, but the sign of the prophet Jonas," Matt. 12:39; 16:4. "And He did not many mighty works there because of their unbelief," Matt. 13:58. When some believed in His name, seeing the miracles which He did, the Lord did not trust them, John 2:23-25. The miracles were intended for those who, basing themselves on Scripture and thus expecting the coming of the Messiah and of the Kingdom, were willing to believe that Jesus was the Christ. They knew, in fact, that this coming would be accompanied by signs and the "powers of the world (age) to come," Heb. 6:5. Those who were not disposed to believe in Him – because they did not believe what the Scriptures said of Him – were always referred to the witness of the written Word, John 5:31-47. (See also Luke 16:31.)[62]

Many of the prophecies already accomplished testified that the Messiah had come. See, for instance, Matt. 21:1-9 and Zech. 6:9. The Lord Himself declares that He is the Christ, Matt. 26:63, 64; (Dan. 7:13); John 5:36. He is the sent one from God, John 13:3; 17:3; Isa. 61:1.

3. Jesus Christ was the King of Israel.

Listen to the witnesses:

> *The three wise men*: "Where is He that is born King of the Jews?" Matt. 2:2.

The angel Gabriel: "and the Lord God shall give unto Him the throne of His father David: and He shall reign over the house of Jacob forever" Luke 1:32, 33.

The prophet Zechariah: "Behold thy King cometh unto thee" Matt. 21:5; John 12:15; Zech. 9:9.

Nathanael: "Thou art the King of Israel" John 1:49.

The multitudes: "Hosanna to the Son of David" Matt. 21:9, "The King of Israel" John 12:13. See also Luke 19:38.

Pilate: "This is Jesus the King of the Jews" Matt. 27:37; Mark 15:26; John 19:19. See also Mark 15:9, 12; John 19:14, 15.

One of the malefactors: "Lord, remember me when thou comest into Thy Kingdom" Luke 23:42.

The Lord Himself: "the Son of man… shall sit upon the throne of His glory: and before Him shall be gathered all nations" Matt. 25:31, 32. "Art thou the King of the Jews? And Jesus said unto him, "Thou sayest" Matt. 27:11; Mark 15:2; Luke 23:39. See also John 18:33-37. This reign is not limited to the hearts of men and does not involve a "Church;" at that time it concerned only Israel.

4. The Kingdom will be on Earth.

And Jerusalem will be its center. This Kingdom is called the "Kingdom of heaven," a name which has led some to assume that this is about a kingdom *in* "heaven" and not on earth; however, this expression indicates its origin and not the locality where it will extend.

Effectively, the Greek text here uses the genitive, and out of numerous texts we mention only Rom. 4:11 and 13 ("of the faith" – "through the faith") to show that either the cause or the origin may be intended by this wording. If one might still be doubtful, because of John 18:36 "My kingdom is not of the world," we could reply that the inspired text says: "My kingdom is not **out of** this world." For the preposition "ek" (out of) is used, showing that this kingdom does not come from this world – as the others – but is of heavenly origin. We have seen, in fact, that God willed – already by the creation of Adam – to realize a kingdom on earth.

This kingdom had been prepared since the "foundation" of the world, Matt. 25:34. It is, therefore, clearly of heavenly origin, though on earth. The "Sermon on the mount" confirms that it is about the earth: "Blessed are the meek: for they shall inherit the earth." Matt. 5:5. The Lord was speaking about earthly things, John 3:12. Jerusalem is the city of the great King, Matt. 5:35.

This kingdom will spread over the entire promised land included from the Nile to the Euphrates, Gen. 15:18. On this subject, we recall the promises of Dan. 2:44; 4:25, 26; 7:13, 14, 27.[63]

The designation "Kingdom of God" is wider than "Kingdom of heaven," for this term, which is also used in Rom. 14:17; 1 Cor. 15:50 and Col. 4:11, indicates in a general manner *all* that relates to the reign of God, whether on earth – where it concerns more specially the "kingdom of heaven" – or concerning the spiritual reign of God within the man who submits to Him. The "kingdom of heaven" is thus included in the "kingdom of God" and is sometimes called by the latter expression, as is often the case in the Gospels of Mark, Luke and John. But it would not be logical to infer from the general term that there will be no earthly kingdom concerning a nation, and to think that there would merely be a spiritual kingdom which would already be in effect in our time. The Lord does not reign effectively over the whole earth, Satan is not yet "bound up," 1 Pet. 5:8, and is still the god of this world, 2 Cor. 4:4. While Matt. 28:18 says that all power has been *given* to the Lord in heaven and earth, the Lord has not yet *taken possession* of His reign; this will only happen when He returns in glory, Rev. 6:16; 11:15, 17; 12:10; 16:1, 6. Besides, should this reign have begun already, it would be impossible to explain how, after some 1900 years, the world still finds itself in the present condition where apostasy, unbelief, and blasphemy are steadily increasing.

Far from teaching a gradual coming of the Kingdom of heaven, the Word of God speaks of a sudden coming: "For as the lightning cometh out of the east, and shineth even to the west; so shall also the coming of the Son of man be." Matt. 24:27; Luke 17:24. Rather than a gradual conversion of the world leading to the Kingdom, the present age will end in an increase in iniquity, Matt. 24:12, and a lack of faith, Luke 18:8.

After the coming of the Antichrist and the great tribulation, the "tribes of the earth" will see the Son of man coming in the clouds of heaven with power and great glory.[64]

We can well understand that one cannot accept the position of certain "chiliasts" who believe that the earthly kingdom is the final goal. But there can be no valid objection if one understands that there will be, simultaneously, other spheres of blessings unrelated to the earth, but which are part of the Kingdom of God, considered in general, and if one understands that the age to come will be followed by that of the new creation, which in turn will lead to the final goal, where God is all in all.

5. Israel had to be converted so the Kingdom could come.

The Kingdom was "near" in those times, it was John the Baptist's basic message: "Repent: for the kingdom of heaven is at hand.", Matt. 4:17. The King was already with them, though not definitively. One thing only was still needed: repentance of the elected people, requested for so long. Note how the Lord insists on conversion in Matt. 18:3. The twelve Apostles also had to proclaim: "The kingdom of heaven is at hand," Matt. 10:7.

However, what is near can also recede. Thus the Lord has never positively stated that the kingdom would come shortly. In Matt. 10:23 He uses the verb "erchomai" in the subjunctive, thus indicating possibility, not certainty. These words will again become applicable at the end of the present age.[65]

6. The approach of the earthly Kingdom was accompanied by visible signs: miracles and the submission of the powers of evil.

As soon as one's attention has been drawn to this fact, it would seem that one must be impressed by such texts as follow: "Preaching the gospel of the kingdom, and healing all manner of sickness and all manner of disease among the people.", Matt. 4:23. "Preaching the gospel of the kingdom, and healing every sickness and every disease among the people.", Matt. 9:35. "The kingdom of heaven is at hand. Heal the sick, cleanse the lepers, raise the dead, cast out devils: freely ye have received, freely give.", Matt. 10:7, 8. "But if I cast out devils by the Spirit of God, then the kingdom of God is come unto you.", Matt. 12:28.

We are limiting our self to Matthew's gospel.

As we have seen, the miracles were intended to be, for those faithful to the Scriptures, a sign of the coming of the Messiah, and thus of the Kingdom. The King has the power necessary to control the powers of nature and to bind the evil spiritual powers. During the Kingdom was to be accomplished what Adam should have accomplished before his fall: subjugate the earth. During the kingdom, then, the conditions on earth will be completely changed; see the prophecies of Isa. 11:1-12; 32:15; 35:6-9; 43:19, 20; 65:19-25; Hosea 2:20-22; Amos 9:11-15. Healings and miracles are among the powers of the age to come, Heb. 6:5, but are not the rule in this present age. The moment that the setting up of the Kingdom and the coming of the Messiah are delayed to a later time – because of Israel's unbelief – *the signs cease*. We will see all this when we review the times of Acts and the present period.

Meanwhile, the reader may realize that texts such as Matt. 10:8 and Mark 16:17, 18 are not applicable to the period in which we live, but rather to the times during which the kingdom is near and when Israel, therefore, must be in their land and be the people of God. If one does not distinguish the things that differ such texts cannot be understood, and one could then be tempted to ignore or eliminate them.[66]

7. Jesus Christ was sent only to the lost sheep of the house of Israel.

"He shall save His People from their sins," Matt. 1:21.

"(He) shall rule My People Israel," Matt. 2:6.

"Go not into the way of the Gentiles, … But go rather to the lost sheep[67] of the house of Israel," Matt. 10:5, 6.

"I am not sent but unto the lost sheep of the house of Israel.", Matt. 15:24.

See also the words addressed to the Syrophenician woman, Mark 7:26, 27.

After having chosen a people who would have the mission to bless the other peoples, God sends them His Son. It was necessary that Israel were first regenerated to be able to serve others.

It is generally understood that a "religion" is a cult rendered to a divinity, based on a particular doctrine. By the Law, God gave the elected people their "religion," which was based on love of God and neighbor,[68] and comprising ceremonies representing spiritual realities, as well as prescriptions for family and social life.

But this Law did not provide the means to accomplish all that God asked of them; to enable them to do this, the New Covenant was needed. It is through faith in Christ, by becoming "Christians," that the Jews – while remaining Jews and forming a nation – could practice their "religion" integrally. There is thus no question that Jesus Christ came "to found a new religion" or to replace Israel by a "Church." The Lord did not come to destroy, but to fulfil the Law and the Prophets, Matt. 5:17. He did not come to protest against the Jews' "religion:" He was a minister of *the circumcision* for the truth of God, to confirm the promises made unto the fathers, Rom. 15:8. This concerns the earthly Abrahamic covenants.

Let us quote here Acts 3:25, 26: "Ye are the children of the prophets, and of the covenant which God made with our fathers, saying unto Abraham, and in thy seed shall all the kindreds of the earth be blessed. Unto *you first* God, having raised up His Son Jesus, sent Him to bless you, in turning away every one of you from his iniquities."

8. In the earthly Kingdom, the twelve Apostles will have a mission relating to Israel.

We have seen that during the times of the Gospels the Apostles were to go only to the lost sheep of Israel. They were to proclaim that the Kingdom was near and that Israel had to repent in order that the Messiah could come in glory. What would their mission be during the Kingdom? The answer is clear: "In the regeneration when the Son of man shall sit in the throne of His glory, ye also shall sit upon twelve thrones, judging the twelve tribes of Israel.", Matt. 19:28; Luke 22:30.

The twelve Apostles to the circumcision, therefore, will be leading[69] the nation of Israel. Had the people repented, this could have taken place in their lifetime, but now, the Apostles will first have to be resurrected.

In any case, it is to them solely that this duty is entrusted, and there can thus be no question of "apostolic succession," one of the many problems arising out of the idea that Israel was replaced by the Church, problems which cause divisions within Christianity.

We can now better understand the well-known text: "And I will give unto thee the keys of the kingdom of heaven: and whatsoever thou shalt bind on earth shall be bound in heaven." Matt. 16:19.[70] The keys are a sign of the power conferred to someone (see Isa. 22:22). This power, furthermore, is not the monopoly of Peter, for it is shared by all the other Apostles to the circumcision, Matt. 18:18; John 20:23.

Let us also look into the duties entrusted to the Apostles after the Lord's resurrection.

We have already touched upon that of Mark 16:15-18. It was given while "they sat at meat," v. 14, and was exercised forthwith, v. 20. It is impossible to exercise it at present, while the Kingdom is not "near" and the Lord does not confirm the preaching of His Word by visible signs.

That of Matt. 28:18-20 was given to the Twelve on another occasion, on a mountain in Galilea. His work having been accomplished, the Lord could say: "All power is given unto Me in heaven and in earth." But we also know that not until the end of this eon will the Kingdom be delivered to the Lord, when He will *seize* His great power and *take possession* of His reign, Rev. 11:15, 17; 12:10; etc. Similarly, Heb. 2:8 says that all things are put under His feet, but adds: "But now we see not yet all things put under Him." God can reign in the hearts of the faithful, but we are still living in the evil age of which Satan is "king."

It is after the return of the Lord, when He will have taken possession of His reign over all the earth, that the Apostles to the circumcision will have to go to all the nations. We recall how many times the Prophets have spoken of the blessings of the nations through Israel.

This will occur under the leadership of the Twelve. Then will begin a world-wide mission, where the missionaries and their children will be immune to diseases, and which will – by the powers which will then be given them – be enormously successful.

During the time of Acts, the Apostles to the circumcision only exceptionally addressed themselves to the nations. And never does Scripture say that they baptized "In the name of the Father, the Son, and the Holy Spirit".[71] It is only during the age to come that it may be said that the Lord will be with them in Person all the days until the end of that age. (See Eze. 43:7; 48:35; Zeph. 3:15-17.)

9. The Church mentioned in the Gospels is made up of Jews faithful to the Lord. It is called the Bride.

One must realize that during the time of the Gospels, and even a little afterwards, the Gentiles are considered as dogs and placed in the same category as publicans and sinners. They were never tolerated in an assembly[72] of Jews, unless they were "proselytes." During the Kingdom, the totality of the Jews who believed in Jesus Christ is also called "ekklesia" or assembly,[73] just as the whole of the people was called "kahal" in Gen. 28:3. It is of this future Church that Matt. 16:18 is speaking: "And I say also unto thee, that thou art Peter, and upon this rock I will build My church."

The words: "the gates of hell shall not prevail against it" relate to the resurrection and thus indicate that this is about a future assembly. Before the Church of the Kingdom can be established, the twelve Apostles must be resurrected; the Hades ("hell") will not have the power to prevent the formation of this Church, for it is Jesus Christ who holds the keys to it.[74]

This Judeo-Christian church is called "the Bride." Already in the OT, the elected people are called "the Bride," "woman," "wife" of the Lord.[75] The parable of Matt. 22 speaks of a marriage during the Kingdom. Jesus Christ is the bridegroom, Matt. 9:15; John 3:29. The marriage of the Lamb is also mentioned in Rev. 19:7; 21:9.

10. Part of what the Lord was asking in the Gospels will have to be performed only by Israel and only when the Kingdom will again be near.

First of all, here is an example showing the necessity of distinguishing the times and the circumstances before following a precept.

During the preaching of the Kingdom, the Twelve were to take with them neither gold, nor silver, nor brass, nor scrip, nor coats, "for the workman is worthy of his meat," Matt. 10:9, 10. But notice the radical change when the representatives of Israel have rejected the message in their land: "But now, he that hath a purse, let him take it, and likewise his scrip: and he that hath no sword, let him sell his garment, and buy one.", Luke 22:36. When the Kingdom is in view, God already is reigning, in principle, and His messengers are not to concern themselves with material needs. But otherwise, one must take care of everything and even defend oneself, with weapons if needed.[76]

One thus sees the very great practical importance of distinguishing the dispensations. There is nothing more disastrous than to try and observe something which is not addressed to us. Let us beware of emulating those of whom the Apostle said: "I bear them record that they have a zeal of God, but not according to knowledge.", Rom. 10:2.

Because of the failure to clearly distinguish the Divine plan and the way of salvation, we see everywhere a tendency to follow that which has been prescribed for Israel in other circumstances, or to appropriate to ourselves the privileges belonging to the elected people. Some believe they are replacing Israel as far as their covenants, missions, and prerogatives are concerned. The Sabbath is observed, as well as part of the visible institutions of this people, where one falsely claims to a right of having special gifts. All this can only discredit the Bible, create divisions and strife, a shameful situation for a Christianity which pretends that the Lord is already reigning on earth.

Without Scriptural doctrine it is impossible to live in accordance with the will of God, to fully appreciate His grace and to glorify Him as He should be.

11. The ceremonies of the Law had to be observed by the Jews, including those who believed in Jesus Christ.

We have shown that the Law, given by God to Moses, required above all to love God and neighbor, and was thus aiming at the heart of man. The ceremonies had no value in themselves, and the Lord abhorred them when they were observed by men with an ill-disposed heart.

The Gospels again draw attention to this inward state of the heart, but never state that external things should no longer be observed by those to whom they were given, i.e. the Jews. On the contrary, those things were to be observed still, as the following texts show:

Matt. 5 and 6 speak of the Law, the temple, offerings, fasting, etc.

Matt. 7 requires nothing other than which is contained in "the law and the prophets."

Matt. 19:17 advises: "keep the commandments."

Matt. 23:23 recalls that "the weightier matters of the law" are judgment, mercy, and faithfulness, but not to the neglect of other things.

Matt. 24:20 shows that the sabbath will still have to be observed in the future.

And we especially remember the words of the Lord: "Think not that I am come to destroy the law, or the prophets: I am not come to destroy, but to fulfil. For verily I say unto you, till heaven and earth pass, one jot or one tittle shall in no wise pass from the law, till all be fulfilled. Whosoever therefore shall break one of these least commandments, and shall teach men so, he shall be called the least in the kingdom of heaven: but whosoever shall do and teach them, the same shall be called great in the kingdom of heaven." Matt. 5:17-19.

The Lord Himself observes the prescriptions of the Law, but not necessarily in the manner in which the doctors of the Law understand it.

Further, we have already seen that the Law and its ceremonies will remain in force during the entire Kingdom period; the Prophets, and particularly Ezekiel, teach us this. The Law will then be written in their hearts, Jer. 31:31-34, that is to say they will delight in it (Rom. 7:22; Ps. 37:31; and all of Ps. 119).

But all men do not have to observe God's commandments in the form in which they were given to Israel. And the Jews can observe them faithfully only in their land and when the Temple is present.

12. Israel will have a world-wide mission.

We have already spoken of this in proposition 8. Under the leadership of the twelve Apostles to the circumcision, Israel will have to evangelize the world; they will have the support of the necessary spiritual powers. The Lord will be with them and will testify of His grace by wonders and miracles, as was already taking place in the times of the Gospels and Acts.

They will be a light to the nations and will carry the salvation of the Lord unto the end of the earth, Isa. 49:6. They will declare the glory of the Lord among the nations, Isa. 66:19. Since Satan will be bound during this time, Rev. 20:2, and the curse over the earth removed, Rom. 8:19-22, their work will be very fruitful.

13. The New Covenant is concluded by the Christ.

We have seen that the Old Covenant promised "eternal life" (life during the eon to come), provided that all the prescriptions of the Law were complied with, and that Israel had committed themselves to practice, by their own efforts, all that the Lord required. This was a commitment whereby the "wife" of the Lord had placed herself "under bondage" of the Law. However, this Law allowed for the case where a wife having bound herself by a pledge, could be freed by her husband, Num. 30:7-9. It is through the New Covenant with the house of Israel and the house of Judah, announced by the Prophets,[77] that the "wife" will be delivered by grace. The Lord will not remember her sin after her repentance.

In all this, Gentiles are not involved. Neither the Old nor the New Covenants are addressed to them. But they will share in the blessings of the New Covenant since it will enable Israel to be a people of priests and spread the Divine blessings over all the earth.

Any covenant required the sprinkling of blood, and without the shedding of blood there is no remission, Ex. 24:8; Heb. 9:20-22. It was the covenant of Jer. 31 which would bring the true Redemption from sins, which would blot out sins. And instead of the symbolic blood of goats and calves, the real blood of the Son of man was needed. This New Covenant could only be concluded, therefore, by the death of Christ, Heb. 9:12.

On the first day of the feast of unleavened bread, Matt. 26:17, the 14th Nisan, Lev. 23:5, at even, the Lord was celebrating the Passover with His disciples, and after the supper, Luke 22:20; 1 Cor. 11:25, He took the cup of blessing,[78] and said: "This cup is the new testament in My blood," 1 Cor. 11:25. Every time they would drink of this cup (at Passover), the Christian Jews would be proclaiming the death of the Lord and consequently the conclusion of the New Covenant.

Thus the Passover, recalling first of all their exodus from Egypt, partook of its full meaning: it spoke of the blood of the Divine Lamb, shed to make the New Covenant which would deliver Israel from sin.

Every year on the 14th of Nisan, Christian Jews were to repeat this testimony, and this as long as the nation had not repented and the Lord had not come in glory. It is quite clear that once their King had come and His Kingdom was established, the Passover, although still celebrated[79]will not be celebrated in the same manner. The Lord said that He would, in His Father's Kingdom, "drink it new" the fruit of the vine. [80] The Passover will then be "fulfilled," Luke 22:16.

But as long as Israel is not the people of God, the Passover could not be celebrated. And this feast, with the ceremonial we have mentioned, cannot be observed by the Gentiles, for the Lord had said to Moses and Aaron; "There shall no stranger eat thereof" (i.e. no one uncircumcised in the flesh).[81]

We deeply regret to upset, perhaps, the religious feelings of our readers. However, we should not fear to be losing anything but human traditions. While the New Covenant was not made with us, our privileges are nevertheless no less considerable. Our blessings – which are not earthly – can go far beyond all that relates to the New Covenant. Thus if our "Church" is not "the wife," we can nevertheless enter into an even closer spiritual communion with the Lord. We can but gain by better understanding the Truth, even if we have "to buy" it, Pro. 23:23, by sacrificing many dearly held practices which turn out to be non-Scriptural.

14. Remission of sins was conditional, and the Prophets already knew this.

To correctly understand the Gospels, it is important not to introduce into them the truths which have been revealed at a later time. To clearly see what must be understood by "the remission of sins," let us above all not consult the Apostle Paul when he is speaking about justification! (We will return later to the difference between the two.) For the moment, let us just learn the significance of the remission of sins by listening to what the Lord and the Prophets have said; that was all that their listeners could know about it and that was enough for them to understand.

The parable of the king and his servants will serve to illustrate, Matt. 18:23-34. First we read that one of the servants owed a great debt which he could not pay; upon his pleading, the king then "forgave" him the debt.[82] But because of the despicable behavior of this servant towards a colleague who owed him a small sum, he is now obliged to repay his debt in full. Here, we see that a "remission" or "forgiveness is not something final, but a conditional grace. It is not the perfect and definitive forgiveness, without works, about which Paul will be speaking in his last Epistles, Eph., Phil., Col., for instance.[83]

The Gospels do not go beyond what the Prophets had already proclaimed.[84] Sin was not blotted out, but "covered," (Rom. 4:7. This is the meaning of the Hebrew word translated by "propitiation") by the blood of animals, in view of the real sacrifice of the "propitiative" Victim, 1 John 2:2; 4:10.

To limit ourselves to the Gospels would be to deprive ourselves from reconciliation and justification, whereby man ceases to be considered as sinner, and where win is not merely "covered," but where man, through his communion with the risen Christ, is dead to sin and just. This matter is further developed in our works *The Teachings of the Apostle Paul* and *The Way of Salvation.*

15. In the Gospels, the goal to be reached along the way of salvation is the new birth.

The OT frequently speaks of the new heart and new spirit that the sons of Israel would receive[85] after their repentance and the forgiveness of their sins. And Eze. 36:25 adds: "Then will I sprinkle clean water upon you, and ye shall be clean."

This is about a regeneration a new birth or "birth from above," a birth of water and of the spirit (i.e. of spiritual water) as in John 3:3-6.

It is after having reached this communion with God that men will be able to love Him with all their heart and do what God desires of them: no longer by their own efforts, but by the power of the Spirit which leads them. (This is discussed in greater detail in *The Way of Salvation.*)

By a national repentance, Israel was to attain a *national* new birth and so bring a world-wide new birth. The age to come, in fact, is designated by the term "new birth."[86]

But the *individual* new birth can occur at any time and is not necessarily accompanied by the signs which will characterize the coming age.

16. The eternal life spoken of in the Gospels is the life on earth, during the coming age, of those who will not die.

We already have briefly commented on the meaning of the Hebrew and Greek words "olam" and "aion" (eon or age). Appendix 1 summarizes a long study on this subject.

It is principally the coming age that the Prophets had in view, the age of the Kingdom on earth; and the life of those who believe in the Lord is the "eonian" life (usual translation: "everlasting").[87]

The Gospels also speak of this life. A comparison between the two following verses show that this life is in relation to the Kingdom on earth, and was prepared since the "foundation" of the world (see Chapter II):

> "...inherit the kingdom prepared for you from the foundation of the world," Matt. 25:34.
> "...the righteous (shall go) into life eternal.", Matt. 25:46.

The following passage shows that it is indeed about the age (eon) to come:

> "Who shall not receive manifold more in this present time, and in the world (age) to come life everlasting," Luke 18:30.

Eonian life refers to the ages through which God achieves His plan, but during which perfection, a perfect communion with God, is not yet attained. It is only after the 5th age that God will be all in all. But, individually, we can already now be placed, through grace, in the corresponding spiritual position, the state of "perfect man, unto the measure of the stature of the fulness of Christ," Eph. 4:13, where Christ is our life, Col. 3:4.

17. Faith in Jesus Christ leads to eonian life.

"He that believeth on [88] Me hath everlasting life," John 6:47. God is the Source of all life; only Christ can give us life fully. As a matter of fact, through spiritual communion with Him, "natural" life can become "eonian" life. God has given us Eonian life, says the Apostle John, 1 John 5:11, and this life is in His Son. Within the sphere of regeneration, this eonian life is earthly; by a closer communion one can obtain the heavenly eonian life, and the final goal will be reached when Christ Himself becomes our life, as indicated above.

As we have seen in the previous proposition, eonian life on earth will only be effectively received in the age to come. Thus in general it is through a resurrection that men partake of it. The Prophets knew of this resurrection (see, for instance, Isa. 26:19; 27:13; Dan. 12:2 and Luke 20:37). Those who are believers in Christ at His coming will be transformed and will not die: "And whosoever liveth and believeth in Me shall never die.", John 11:25, 26. This is the resurrection "at the last day," John 6:40; 11:24, that is to say, at the last day of our age, just before "the world (age) to come," Luke 20:35; Heb. 6:5. It is a resurrection "out of the dead" (Mark 12:25; Luke 20:35, Greek text) because other dead will only be resurrected at the end of the age to come. Later on Paul tells us that there will be a resurrection where justified men will be caught up together in the clouds to meet the Lord in the air at His coming in glory.[89] Finally, there will also be an "out-resurrection out of the dead" according to the Greek text of Phil. 3:11, for those who will appear with Christ, Col. 3:4.

18. Israel was not rejected after they had crucified their Messiah, but could still repent and accept the forgiveness offered them.

Forgiveness based on atonement was known by Israel, Num. 15:27-31. When the True sacrifice was about to be offered, the Divine Victim said: "Father, forgive them; for they know not what they do.", Luke 23:34. The Lord was thereby stating – and we must therefore accept it – that they sinned "in ignorance" and not "presumptuously" (or "with a high hand"). According to the Law they could therefore be forgiven. And if we believe that the Son of God's prayers are granted, the forgiveness of Israel is not to be doubted.

The Apostle Peter could thus say: "And now, brethren, I wot that through ignorance ye did it, as did also your rulers" and he adds: "Repent ye therefore, and be converted, that your sins may be blotted out, when the times of refreshing shall come from the presence of the Lord; And He shall send Jesus Christ, which before was preached unto you.", Acts 3:17, 19.

It is thus quite certain that the elected people was not yet rejected as such during the period of Acts.

19. After the ascension the disciples were to wait for the power of the Spirit announced by the Prophets and by the Lord.

Let us cite just the following passages from the Prophets: "I will pour My spirit upon thy seed," Isa. 44:3. "A new heart will I give you, and a new spirit will I put within you," Eze. 36:26.

The Lord has said to the disciples: "I send the promise of My Father upon you; but tarry ye in the city of Jerusalem, until ye be endued with power from on high.", Luke 24:49. And Acts 1:5 adds: "For John truly baptized with water; but ye shall be baptized with the Holy Ghost not many days hence."

We will see later how these prophecies had begun to be realized at Pentecost and that, there also, it concerned Israel.

e. The Cross and Resurrection

In our brief review we have seen that God had created a creature who was good but who turned away from Him, that God then provided a means for restoration: Adam, but in this case also the creature again missed its goal. Finally, God chose a people to arrive at a rebirth, to a Kingdom on earth, to a new creation, and finally to the ultimate goal: God all in all.

From "the Law and the Prophets" this people knew that, one day, the Anointed One, the Messiah, the Christ, would come, and indeed this extraordinary event occurred: The Son of God came not only as Mediator to create, but took upon Him the form or a Servant to save. Everything was ready: the people, the land, the City, the King. But, as always, the purposes of God are to be accomplished in freedom. God offers, enables, and the creature must accept, execute. One more thing was required: having learned through experience their powerlessness and their state of sin, the Jews, being led to Christ by the Law, were to accept this Messiah as their Savior. But once more comes the fall: that part of the elected people who are in the land reject their Messiah. Is this the end of everything? No, Divine grace is not exhausted, the impossible is accomplished. Already "ordinary man," the Son humiliates Himself unto death, even the death at the cross. This is a nonsense to natural man, a scandal for the Jews, an incomprehensible event for the disciples. Is this Satan's final victory? Has he succeeded in destroying the posterity of the woman? No, this is the sublime solution to the impossible-to-resolve problem: how can a God of Love be at the same time a God of Justice, how can a sinner be justified?

In *The Way of Salvation,* we take a closer look at the work of our Lord Jesus Christ. His blood has not only sealed the New Covenant with Israel, but leads to reconciliation and justification, and can blot out sin in the world and give peace and Life to all.

By his resurrection from out of the dead, Jesus Christ has been declared with power to be the Son of God. The liberating sacrifice was accomplished, the Messiah was living, and grace abounded. The time of Acts thus permitted strong and decisive witnessing to the elected people.

But although the Lord Jesus is the Christ from the national point of view of the people of Israel, He is also a personal Redeemer. The individual creature, spiritually separated from God, must learn not to take itself as center, to die to itself and return to the Source of all good. But how can this goal be achieved? Its lack of communion with God prevents the creature from entering the way of salvation.

However, its likeness to the Image of God is not completely erased; its reason is darkened but can still enable it on the one hand to know God through the visible things and to glorify Him as Creator, and on the other hand to realize that it must turn to Him. Following such a conversion, God may restore the spiritual communion with this individual creature, make it born again enlighten it by His Spirit.

But this creature still remains in its state of sin, a consequence of its belonging to the Adamic humanity. However, a new humanity now has been formed, with Jesus Christ as origin, the second Adam. Having lowered Himself down to the humanity of Adam, He died to this rebellious humanity, and through His resurrection has begun to form a new humanity, righteous before God. Thus, the bridge is established, the way is open, a complete return is possible. Only one condition must be satisfied: communion with Him. While all men are by birth in communion with Adam and are therefore under sin, communion with Christ must be accepted individually through faith. One has then died with Christ and is justified from sin.

To summarize the way of salvation: man can, by his natural faculties, recognize God within creation, become conscious of his weakness and freely turn to his Creator. God can then, by a spiritual rebirth, give him the necessary spiritual faculties to understand spiritual things and to come into communion with the second Adam through faith. Man can then die to his old humanity and live in Christ in the new humanity.

f. The period of the Acts of the Apostles

If one should forget that the Lord has been first of all the Servant of the circumcised ones, and that He came to confirm and accomplish the promises made to the fathers of Israel, then the Gospels will be misunderstood and the period of the Acts will be largely misinterpreted.

And so, it is precisely upon these false interpretations that are based all the theologies, more or less developed, of the "Christian" denominations and religious sects. We believe that the present chaos within Christianity is mainly the inevitable consequence of this fundamental error. Nearly all that has divided – and still divides – Christians, has its roots in errors of interpretation of Acts: baptism, various ceremonies, spiritual gifts, sabbaths and legalisms, false millennialism, destructive criticism, etc. The moment one realizes that Israel is not rejected as God's people, one must revise one's entire theological system.

We do not presume to completely clarify the events of this important period, nor to be presenting the absolute truth; but we will present a few points of view concerning Acts which will prove to adequately prevent any major divergence from the truth and which might serve as the starting point for a synthesis of all the data given in the Bible, a synthesis which will approach the Truth.

In this endeavor, we will try not to introduce any preconceived idea, any unjustifiable human tradition. Remembering the teachings of the OT and of the Gospels, we will examine afresh the book of Acts and try to find out if we are faced with the continuation of that which precedes it, or if it signals the beginning of a new order of things.

We believe this examination would be clearer by presenting it in terms of a series of propositions, but we emphasize that these propositions have not been determined by any "*a priori*," and then turning to the Scriptures to prove their validity. Rather, these propositions result from a "scientific" study where the written Word of God was the only absolute norm, and where we have sacrificed any idea which could not be justified by it.

1. The Apostles awaited and proclaimed the Kingdom for Israel.

Let us put ourselves in the Apostles shoes. They were aware, through the Scriptures, of all the promises made to Israel in relation with the earthly Kingdom. They had heard their Lord say that the Kingdom was near and that its actual coming could be realized providing that the elected people did repent. They had seen the miraculous signs indicating its proximity. Furthermore, two events of major importance which concerned them personally had already taken place:

1. The Lord "had opened their understanding, that they might understand the Scriptures," Luke 24:45.
2. The Lord had spoken to them for forty days about the things pertaining to the Kingdom of God, Acts 1:3.

It is in this frame of mind that the Apostles asked the Lord: "wilt thou at this time restore again the kingdom to Israel?" Acts 1:6. Consequently, there is no doubt that they were not thinking about a "spiritual" kingdom, and that they could be expecting the impending setting up of the earthly Kingdom of heaven, which had always been foretold as being near.[90]

Had they been mistaken about such a serious matter the Lord would most certainly have corrected them; but He does not reproach them for being in error. He simply says that it is not for them to know *the times*. We, who know that the Kingdom – so near at the time – was to be rejected by Israel during the time of Acts, are able to understand why the Lord could not give them an answer as to the time.

Because then He would have had to tell them that, in reality, this Kingdom would be delayed for long centuries because of the "hardening" of Israel; this would certainly have weakened their witnessing during the time of Acts and would also have diminished the responsibility of the people. The Kingdom was effectively near, and they were to proclaim it as such, not knowing whether Israel would or would not repent. Only God knew which way the people would react, and He alone knew the *time*. It is not always good for man to know certain things.

We will see that this justifiable expectation of the Kingdom on earth persisted during the times of Acts, and in our second proposition we will mention many signs indicating that it was still near.

Early in Acts we see Peter using "the keys" of the Kingdom to bring his people to repentance, Acts 2:38; 3:19. This repentance was the last remaining condition to be satisfied in order for Jesus Christ to come down from heaven in the same manner that they had seen Him go into heaven, Acts 1:11.

All the Apostles were announcing the good news that Jesus was the Christ (Acts 5:42; 8:5, 12; 17:3; 18:5, 28), that is, the Anointed One, the King-Prophet-Priest. As we will see later on, for a long time they addressed themselves only to the Jews because Israel had to go through a national repentance before the Messiah would come in glory, and only then would all the families on earth be blessed through Israel, Acts 3:25.

This message was accompanied by a Divine witnessing, by powers of the age to come: miracles, wonders, and signs. Later, Paul also proclaims the Kingdom to Israel, but afterwards turns to the Gentiles with a new message, as we will see later on.

2. Signs announcing the Kingdom of heaven were numerous during the time of Acts.

Since the age to come was still near, the "powers of the world to come," Heb. 6:5, abounded. God had previously witnessed to Jesus of Nazareth by miracles, wonders and signs, Acts 2:22. Now this same witness accompanied the disciples through the power they had received from the Holy Spirit (Acts 1:8). Thus, in Acts 3:2-13 we see that the healing of a lame man was performed through Divine power to the glory of the

Servant of God. In Acts 5:15, 16, Peter's shadow suffices to heal the sick; evil spirits were subdued, Acts 8:7; 16:16-18; 19:12.

God also wrought special miracles by the hand of Paul, Acts 19:11, 12, right through to near the end of the time of Acts, Acts 28:4-9. The promises of Mark 16:17, 18 were being realized literally.

Even the angels intervene, and show that they are spirits in God's service, sent to minister to those who shall be heirs of salvation, Heb. 1:14. They open prison doors, Acts 5:19; 12:7-10, lead and assist the disciples,[91] and render justice, Acts 12:23. One of the characteristics of the coming age is, indeed, immediate justice; no long delays as at present. The guilty of that age are inexcusable and are punished instantly. The cases of Ananias and Sapphira, Acts 5:5, 10, of Herod, Acts 12:23, and of the sorcerer Barjesus, Acts 13:11, are well known. The forces of nature are at the service of men, Acts 16:26, as will be the rule during the Kingdom, Rom. 8:19-22.

All these Divine testimonies gave complete assurance to God's servants,[92] and the gifts of the spirit enabled them to know those they were speaking to, making possible an effective work far exceeding purely human efforts.

It is evident that in our own time we know nothing of all this. When we observe how all those special phenomena relate to Israel and the Kingdom on earth, we are no longer surprised not to see them in our era where Israel has been temporarily rejected and the Kingdom is no longer near. We notice that Israel is the key to many problems, and that many difficulties disappear the moment we accept the Word literally and simply.

It is rather striking that Paul's epistles written after the setting aside of Israel (Ephesians, Philippians, Colossians, and 2 Timothy do not mention any miracles. On the contrary, Paul, who in Acts was making special miracles, cannot heal Epaphroditus, Phil 2:27, and leaves Trophimus sick at Miletum., 2 Tim. 4:20,[93] Nor does he disdain doctors, for he calls Luke "the beloved physician," Col. 4:14.

No longer do we read about angels, about the power of demons, about immediate justice, about the nearness of the Kingdom; and Paul is abandoned by all (2 Tim. 1:15).[94] This change is so obvious that the critics find this to be a basis for denying the inspiration of all that the Apostle has written and point to the difference between Paul's later teachings with that of Christ and the Twelve.

3. Repentance of the Jewish nation is still the condition required for the coming of the Lord in glory.

In this connection, nothing is changed, although the Messiah had come in humility, sacrificed Himself, and everything should have led the people of Israel to repentance and to turning to its Savior. Let us note a few appeals:

> "Repent, and be baptized everyone of you in the name of Jesus Christ for the remission of sins, and ye shall receive the gift of the Holy Ghost. For the promise is unto you." Acts 2:38-39.

Verse 36 shows that this applies to "all the house of Israel." "Repent ye therefore, and be converted, that your sins may be blotted out, when the times of refreshing shall come from the presence of the Lord; and He shall send Jesus Christ, which before was preached unto you: Whom the heavens must receive until the times of restitution of all things, which God hath spoken by the mouth of all his holy prophets since the world began." Acts 3:19-21.

Let us note that these words were addressed to the "men of Israel" who had delivered up and denied Jesus Christ, verses 12 and 13.

The individual repentance of thousands of Jews was not enough: what was required was a national, official repentance of the religious representatives of the people. An Evangelist minister of our times would have been well satisfied with the results obtained during Acts and also at the time of the final meeting of Paul with the chiefs of the Jews at Rome, many of whom were brought to the faith, Acts 28:17-24. But this does not prevent Paul from pronouncing the sentence of Isa. 6:9, 10.

After so much forbearance and patience, the adulterous wife was rejected, at least for a time. If she had repented, *all* the prophecy of Joel would have been realized and the Day of the Lord would have come, Joel 2:31, 32.

4. **The Law with all its ceremonies, and the circumcision must be observed by the Christian Jews as long as the people of Israel are reckoned as the people of God.**

We have seen, in our proposition 11 above which relates to the times of the Gospels, that the Lord had not come to abolish the Law or the Prophets, but to accomplish it, and that not one iota will disappear from the Law, even during the coming age. We have also seen that, according to the Prophets, circumcision of the flesh, offerings, and other ceremonies will remain in force during the Kingdom. If the period of Acts could have led to the Kingdom, we should expect to find indications to the fact that the Law still had to be observed, even by Christian Jews. Let us examine the texts.

First, we find a series of statements proving that the Jewish feasts were observed by the Apostles and other Christian Jews. Thus, for Pentecost we have: Acts 2:1; 18:21; 20:16; for the days of unleavened bread: Acts 20:6; for the sabbaths, see Appendix 4. Christian Jews were still attending the Temple, Acts 2:42-46; 3:1; 5:20; 21:26; and the synagogue, Acts 13:14, 15; 14:1, etc. They observed fasting, Acts 13:2, and practiced the laying of hands, Acts 6:6; 13:3, etc.

The case of Cornelius, Acts 10:1-33, is very instructive. He was a devout man, fearing God, giving much alms and praying to God continually. Was this model believer highly esteemed within the "Church?" No! On the contrary, Peter considers him as a thing "common" and "unclean," and it needed a vision three times repeated and the intervention of an angel before Peter, the Jew, entered the house of Cornelius, the Gentile. And afterwards, Peter excused himself profusely to the circumcised for having met with the uncircumcised and eaten with them, Acts 11:2-18. Thus we see how fastidious were the Christian Jews, the Apostles at their head, in their rigorous observance of the Law.

It might perhaps be pointed out that the story related in Acts 15 shows, nevertheless, that circumcision of the flesh and the law no longer had to be observed by Christians. As a matter of fact, the question raised there was the following: did non-Jewish believers have to be circumcised in order to be incorporated into the elected people, Ex. 12:43-49, and thereby be able to observe the Law given to the Jews in order to be saved? The answer was negative; did not the Prophets speak of the blessings of the nations through Israel, Acts 15:17? Non-Jewish Christians, therefore, had to form nations separated from Israel. Thus they did not have to be circumcised in the flesh and be incorporated into Israel. However, some recommendations were given, valid only for that time, in order to permit a certain communion between Christian Jews and the non-Jews.[95]

What does this text show? First, that non-Jewish Christians did not have to be circumcised in the flesh, nor observe the Law as it was given to Israel. Then, that Christian Jews did observe the circumcision and the Law – for any discussion about the circumcision of the Gentiles would have been pointless if the Jews themselves were no longer practicing them.

Thus, **twenty years after Pentecost**, a "general council" which gathered the Apostles and the elders in Jerusalem, Jews all of them, shows that Christian Jews were still faithfully observing the Law.

It seems quite clear to us: the Law was not abolished by Christ.[96]

A false interpretation of the Gospels and Acts leads critics to blame the Apostles for many things: "they should not have asked about the restoration of the Kingdom, Acts 1:6;" "they should not have chosen Matthias as the twelfth Apostle, and certainly not by casting lots, Acts 1:26:" "they would have been slack about all that concerned circumcision, Acts 15;" etc. But it is Paul, especially, who is the target. He is criticized for: -his trip to Jerusalem (Acts 21 and Appendix 6), his insistence in saying that he is a Jew, Acts 22:3, a Pharisee, Acts 23:6, and Roman citizen, Acts 22:25, for having a vow, Acts 18:18, and especially for making an offering, Acts 21:26. We can certainly understand that all these actions create an embarrassing situation for those who believe that the Church, the body of Christ of which He Himself is the Head, began at Pentecost. But how can one dare to charge the Apostles with such serious errors? We recall that they had already received the Holy Ghost before Pentecost, John 20:22, that their understanding had been opened that they might understand the Scriptures, Luke 24:45, and finally, that they had been instructed during forty days by the Lord, Acts 1:3.

One could, of course, sacrifice the full inspiration of the Scriptures and the authority of the Apostles in favor of the human notions of what is called the Church. But if one does not wish to do this nor be faced with a mass of obstacles, would it not be better to re-examine traditional notions, and particularly the question of Israel?

The reader will no doubt appreciate how all the problems resulting from many current notions actually become a confirmation of our point of view: that the Christian Jews must observe the Law as long as they are considered to be God's people. Paul's testimony to this matter is clear and conclusive. Several thousands of Jerusalem Jews, under the bishopric of James, the Lord's brother, believed in Christ and were zealous of the Law. Since they had learned – from false brethren, Gal.2:4 – that it was rumored that Paul was teaching all the Jews of the Diaspora to forsake Moses, i.e. the Law, the Apostle to the Gentiles followed the advice of James and the elders, and demonstrated by a ceremony of purification and offerings that those rumors *were false and that he was presenting himself as one obeying the Law,* Acts 21:17-26. He confirmed several times that he was faithful to the Law, Acts 24:17-19; 25:8; 28:17. And nowhere does Scripture suggest that he ever talked or acted against Divine will.

But, it may be objected, how is it possible that Christians could still offer sacrifices? Is not Jesus Christ The only real Sacrifice? Undoubtedly, but the symbol may just as well follow as precede the realization in time of this Sacrifice. For there were – and will be in the future, during the Kingdom – many people who needed to be led to Christ by these symbols.

One thing, however, has changed: it is *the manner* in which sacrifices are offered. While those Jews who did not believe in Christ made offerings under the yoke of the Law, Christians are delivered from this yoke and observe the entire Law through love and certain ceremonies as remembrances of the work of Christ.[97]

Let us note that we have not had to appeal to particular inspired texts; on the contrary, we have taken them simply as they presented themselves, taking into account the smallest details. We have also not selected a few texts, omitting any which might conflict with our interpretation. We have found neither contradictions nor difficulties, apart from that of abandoning our personal ideas and those of non-Scriptural traditions. We have not had to charge the Apostles or the disciples of making errors. We sacrifice only one thing: that which is not confirmed by the Word of God.

But let us carry on with our research and see if it will reinforce our conclusions.

5. Pentecost is the beginning of the realization of the promises to the Jews. The Gentiles begin to be blessed only long afterwards.

Let us first recall propositions 7 and 9 under IVd, "The Gospels.": "Jesus Christ had been sent only to the lost sheep of the house of Israel" and "The Church of the Gospels is made up of Jews faithful to the Lord."

We must now examine this state of things and see if it is radically changed at Pentecost. The above propositions already show that this is not the case, but we will establish this again, independently.

That is about promises given to the Jews is proved as follows:

1) The Lord had told them to "wait for the promise of the Father," Acts 1:4, that is, the "power from on high," Luke 14:49.

2) Those events were a beginning of the realization of the prophecies concerning Israel: "But this is that which was spoken by the prophet Joel." (Acts 2:16; Joel 2:28-31; Isa. 44:3; Eze. 36:36; etc.).[98] And Joel was speaking about the land of the people of Israel.

3) Peter tells "all the house of Israel" that "the promise is unto you, and to your children, and to all that are afar off," Acts 2:36, 39. (Those who are afar off are the Jews of the dispersion, who are also part of "all the house of Israel.") The fact that no Gentile was present at the events of Pentecost results from the following:

   - Pentecost is a Jewish feast, Lev. 23:14-16, and the Jews could not defile themselves by mixing with the uncircumcised.
   - The texts mention only Jews.[99]
   - The first Gentile is mentioned in Acts 8:27, and even then it is made quite clear that he was a proselyte of the Jews. Circumcised proselytes were admitted into the Temple and the synagogue; non-circumcised proselytes did not have those privileges, but the Jews could have dealings with them.
   - The story of Cornelius (already mentioned in proposition 4) shows that Peter had no dealings with Gentiles, <u>even some 10 years after Pentecost.</u> Those

of the circumcision were astonished because of the gift of the Holy Ghost was poured out on the Gentiles also, Acts 10:45. Any question about the presence of Gentiles at Pentecost thus does not even arise.

-   Ten years after Pentecost the Christian Jews of the dispersion preached the Word "to none but unto the Jews only," Acts 11:19.
-   Paul and Barnabas announced the Word of God first to the Jews, and only turned to the Gentiles after the Jews thrust it away. Thus, the blessings which should have come to the Gentiles through Israel, could now come to them directly.

For all these reasons, it is clear that the events of Pentecost agree entirely with our above conclusions, and that they do not indicate an abandonment of the elected People nor the starting point of a universal Church comprised of Jews and Gentiles.[100] What is new is the realization of the ancient promises, and the first signs of the formation of the Church, Matt. 16:18, a church which will blossom during the coming age. It is only a long time after Pentecost that Paul opens up the sphere of the Abrahamic heavenly blessings to Gentiles and Jews. One also realizes that the two loaves of Lev. 23:17 represent Israel and Judah, not Israel and the Gentiles.

6.   The Apostle Paul is not included among the Twelve.

It may be thought to be of little significance whether Paul was or was not included among the Twelve. Yet, something which may appear not to be worth the time to examine it often turns out to have major consequences.

We have already examined, under Section 2.8, concerning the time of the Gospels: "The twelve Apostles will have a mission relative to Israel during the Kingdom on earth." But Paul is especially The Apostle to the Gentiles[101] and is contrasted with the Twelve Apostles to the circumcision in Gal. 2:8, 9. But this does not prevent him to first of all addressing himself to the Jews[102].

As noted earlier, the eleven have sometimes been reproached for not having chosen Paul as the twelfth, rather than Matthias. But it is a fact that the Holy Spirit has led the author of Acts to speak about the Twelve a long time before the conversion of Saul, Acts 2:14; 6:2; and Paul differentiates himself from the Twelve, 1 Cor. 15:5-9. Let us add that the Apostles did not choose Matthias.[103] The correct number was already established and in accordance with Divine will.

While the Twelve were called by the Lord *before* His rejection, Paul and others, such as Barnabas, Acts 14:14, Silvanus and Timotheus, 1 Thess. 1:1; 2:6, Andronicus and Junia, Rom. 16:7, were called by the Lord *after* His Ascension.[104]

All that Paul had learned came directly from the mouth of the Lord, Acts 22:14, Gal. 1:18-20, and not from men. Not before three years have gone by does he communicate with the Twelve.

This enables us to better understand that the messages from the Twelve only concern us in part and indirectly,[105] while those of Paul after he turns away from the Jews concerns all men, individually. All Scripture is inspired and useful, but all is not addressed to all indiscriminately.[106]

To correctly understand the path taken by the Lord in restoring creation, it is important to see that Paul does not have the same ministry as the Twelve. It is to him alone that were revealed a series of "mysteries," i.e. hidden things concerning the realization of God's purposes. He is entrusted with new "economies," or "dispensations," and advances along the way of salvation towards the goal to be attained: identification with Christ, God all in all.

It is very useful as well as very necessary to listen to the individual message concerning the new birth, but one must not stop there. The Twelve will have a world-wide mission in the future; Paul has an individual mission for today and a universal mission for later on.

Let us add that one must exercise care when speaking of "apostolic" teaching when referring to the Twelve, and that an "apostolic" Church based on Peter has actually no Scriptural significance. It is during the Kingdom that the Lord will build a Church based on the Twelve, composed of Christian Jews and forming a visible unity. Its formation, begun at Pentecost, may be resumed during the last times of the present age, but will be fully realized after resurrection, when the Twelve will be living again.

7. The Apostle Paul has proclaimed several Good News during Acts, in particular that of reconciliation, which surpasses that of the New Birth.

Paul announces, as the Twelve were doing, the Kingdom of God to the Jews, Acts 19:8; 28:23, etc.; everywhere he addresses himself first to the Jews. But when the official representatives of the nation reject the Kingdom, he turns to the Gentiles. We learn that this has happened, among other places, at Antioch, acts 13:46, 47, at Corinth, Acts 18:6, and finally at Rome, Acts 28:17-28.

By this, he is showing that God was willing to use Israel to accomplish His purposes concerning the nations in general, but that He would not be hindered by them. Salvation became accessible to the Gentiles directly, in order that the elected nation be provoked to jealousy, Rom. 11:11. Paul then goes beyond the new birth and speaks of justification by faith, Acts 13:39, and he recalls that Abraham was justified before God in this manner, Rom. 4:3; Gal. 2 and 3. This is about the posterity and the heavenly blessings which we have already mentioned at the beginning of this chapter. Paul goes beyond the earthly Kingdom and opens up a new dispensation which will attain its fullness only in the age of the New Creation which must follow the age of the Kingdom on earth. (See sketch on page 119.)

Thus, he gives us a better understanding of the mystery of Christ, i.e. the manner in which God will reach His goal. In the Epistles he wrote during Acts he exposes all that concerns justification and the new creation. He passes on from the old Adamic humanity to the new humanity of Christ.

But the Apostles to the circumcision remain in the old creation and the earthly blessings: their mission is to first of all bring Israel to the new birth, and then, through Israel, the whole earth. Thus they do not yet speak of the sphere of heavenly blessings, of justification before God, of reconciliation.

During the time of Acts, Paul thus makes known in more detail that which had already been made known in general terms by the Prophets. For one must remember that, as a matter of fact, not only the gospel of the Kingdom and the blessings of the nations through Israel, but also the heavenly blessings in relation with Abraham (Heb. 11:16; 12:22) were things that were not hidden.[107]

In our work *The Teachings of the Apostle Paul* we examine in some detail the different messages and missions of Paul as expressed in his Epistles. We show that in the Epistles written *after* Acts 28:28, Paul makes known[108] things which had always been hidden in God: it is about the *great* mystery, the Church which constitutes not only a "body" belonging to Christ, but which is **the** Body of which Christ Himself is the Head. To the individual believer, a new sphere of blessings is now already open, a sphere which corresponds to the final state of creation: God all in all.

Thus Paul's gospel is a complete Gospel.

8. Paul warns against the pernicious teachings of persons who arise out of the midst of believers.

He says, to the elders of the church of Ephesus: "For I know this, that after my departing shall grievous wolves enter in among you, not sparing the flock. Also of your own selves shall men arise, speaking perverse things, to draw away disciples after them. Therefore, watch, and remember, that by the space of three years I ceased not to warn every one night and day with tears." (Acts 20:29-31). We understand then, how great the danger was.

In his Epistles we read: "For such are false apostles, deceitful workers, transforming themselves into the Apostles of Christ. And no marvel; for Satan himself is transformed into an angel of light. Therefore, it is no great thing if his ministers also be transformed as the ministers of righteousness..." (2 Cor. 11:13-15).

One must therefore be extremely prudent. Some claim to follow the teachings of "Jesus," and first-century ideas, pretend to possess special gifts, appear to have an impeccable morality, etc. But they do not hold on to the inspired Word of God, in its integrity and rightly divided; in short, they have no Scriptural doctrine.[109] And so, under cover of what may perhaps be good, but misapplied or insufficient, they set aside that which is essential.

On the other hand, by not correctly distinguishing the ages, the dispensations, - in general 'the things which differ' – one is brought to criticize the inspired Word, to find errors and contradictions everywhere, to deny the full inspiration of the Scriptures.

It is particularly near the end of his life that Paul warns against those whose word "will eat as doth a canker" (2 Tim. 2:16, 17), against those who have "a form of godliness, but denying the power thereof" (1 Tim. 3:1-5), against "evil men and seducers" who deceive and are deceived (2 Tim. 3:13, against those who turn their ears away from the truth and turn to fables (2 Tim. 4:3, 4).

But there is more. It came to be that Paul himself was abandoned, not by unbelievers, but by Christians; not by a few, but by many, even "all they which are in Asia" (2 Tim. 1:15; also Phil. 2:20, 21; Col. 4:11; 2 Tim. 4:16).

Here is something which is completely at variance with what is sometimes said about the spiritual perfection of first-century Christians! We examine this situation in greater detail in *The Teachings of the Apostle Paul.*

9. The entire Jewish Nation is rejected, for a time, at the end of the Acts period.

In the proposition 7 we have seen that the official representatives of Israel had rejected the Kingdom message successively at Antioch, Corinth, and Rome (and before this, there was, of course, the rejection at Jerusalem which was the cause of the crucifixion of the Messiah).

The Kingdom gospel had thus been proclaimed to those of the dispersion as well as to those in the land. The time of Acts thus shows the patience and the forbearance of God toward His people. Even after the cross, all was not lost for them.

But finally, sentence is passed. The dramatic words of Isaiah in Isa. 6:9, 10, after so many years of patience, and which were followed by the captivity of Israel in Assyria, were repeated by the Lord, Matt. 13:14, John 12:40, after He was rejected by the Jewish nation at Jerusalem, and finally by Paul in Acts 28:26, 27. A few years later, in the year 70, the judgment was physically confirmed by the destruction of Jerusalem and the Temple.

Suddenly, all that indicated the proximity of the Kingdom disappeared: no longer a People, no land, no city, no signs, no realization of the prophecies. And, together with Israel, the fulfillment of the Law and the worship instituted by God ended, for all organizations and visible things were related to Israel.

But there remained the messages of Paul concerning invisible things, and he was soon to write his last Epistles making known all the riches of Divine grace, by which man is not only regenerated and justified, but has access to all spiritual blessings in the "above-heavens," being placed there in Jesus Christ at the right hand of God. The visible earthly organization is replaced by a perfect invisible Organism: the Body of which the glorified Christ Jesus is the Head. It is the dispensation of grace *par excellence,* where pure faith replaces the signs. Thus, by the great Mystery would Paul make known the complete way of salvation and so fulfill the Word of God, Col. 1:15.

However, as we have seen, Israel is not set aside forever. The Lord does not break His covenant with them, Lev. 26:44. And so we find Paul speaking of their restoration, Rom. 11:15, and of their salvation, Rom. 11:26; for the gifts and calling of God remain without change, Rom. 11:29.

g. Summary of the Times of the Gospels and Acts

Our propositions, which follow simply from the Scriptures, show that all that happened during the times of the Gospels and of Acts was the beginning of the realization of the prophecies. Long ago God had prepared everything in view of the coming of the Kingdom on earth. He had chosen a people, had brought them into the promised land of which Jerusalem was to be the seat of the theocratic government. The King Himself came to His people, not yet in glory but in humility. Israel, instructed by the Law, should have received Him as their savior Messiah, especially so because this King had announced that the Kingdom was near and confirmed His message by various signs. Thus would Israel have been brought to a national new birth and would have been able to hold their position in the world and, under the leadership of the twelve Apostles, be a blessing to all the nations.

But the representatives of the people are hardened, reject their Messiah at Jerusalem, and have Him crucified. There remained those of the dispersion. For the People were not yet set aside as People of God, but could be forgiven because they did not know what they were doing. The Twelve, and the Apostles called by the Lord after His resurrection, therefore address themselves to the Diaspora, with God confirming their witness by miracles and powers, signs of the proximity of the Kingdom. The power from above, promised to Israel, already comes over many of the faithful: the era of the new birth is virtually beginning. If the people but repent, the Messiah, already resurrected, would come in glory to take possession of His Kingdom. This message is also successively rejected in the great centers.

Meanwhile, Paul receives new revelations about the spiritual blessings promised to Abraham and his heavenly posterity before the circumcision. The elected people's disobedience delays the realization of the Divine plan concerning the regeneration of the world by means of this people. But God is not stopped by man's failure. Through Paul, He already opens up, for individual believers, a sphere of spiritual blessings which will spread and flourish over the entire world during the age of the new creation, i.e. after the age of the Kingdom on earth. Thus the Divine graces can begin to reach all the nations directly, without the medium of Israel.

Up to the end of Acts, Israel remains God's people and, therefore, is not replaced by a new "church." The fact that the heavenly message, which includes reconciliation and justification, is already addressed to all men is no proof that the elected nation is rejected; on the contrary it serves to drive Israel, through jealousy, to accept their privileges.[110]

As long as Israel has not been set aside, the Jews – even those who believe in Christ – must observe all the prescriptions of the Law. But they escape the burden of the Old Covenant, i.e. the duty to satisfy all the commandments by their own efforts. They can now participate in the New Covenant which enables them to do the will of God by the grace which is offered them in Jesus Christ. The blood of the Lamb has sealed this Covenant.

Finally, after the representatives of the Jews of the dispersion have also rejected, at Rome, the Good News of the Kingdom, Israel ceases, for a time, to be God's people.

Here is an incredible event! For about 2000 years God had trained them to become instruments for the work of restoration of the world. All the nations had been placed in the background. To Israel belonged the adoption, the glory, the Covenants, the worship, the promises, the Fathers, the Christ, Rom. 9:4, 5. The entire burden of restoration was laid upon them. What event, then, could have had greater impact throughout the world than the rejection of this people at the end of the Acts period?

The following sketch illustrates the contrasts between the conditions during Acts and those of the present period.

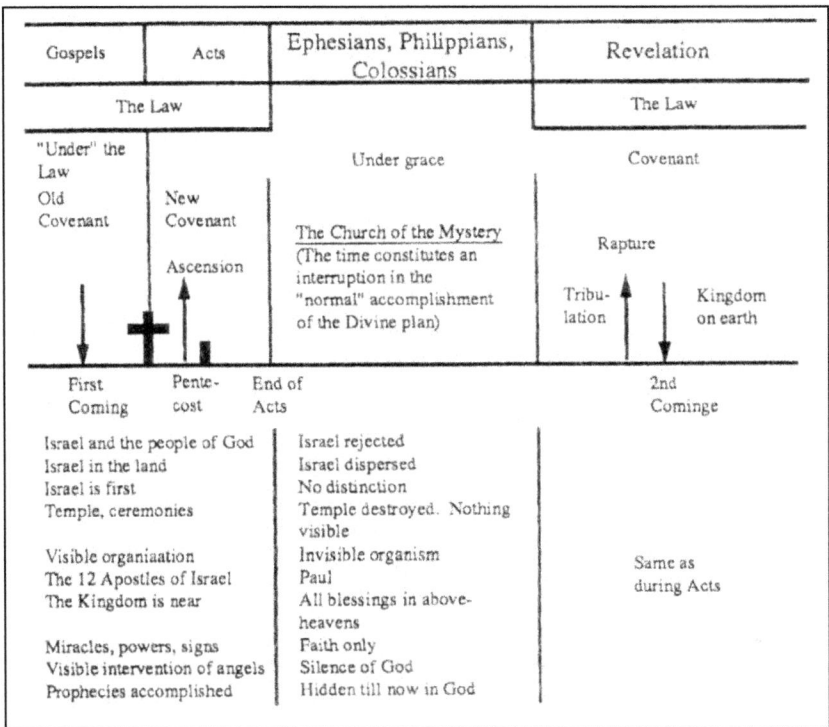

Gospels	Acts	Ephesians, Philippians, Colossians	Revelation
The Law			The Law
"Under" the Law Old Covenant	New Covenant Ascension	Under grace The Church of the Mystery (The time constitutes an interruption in the "normal" accomplishment of the Divine plan)	Covenant Rapture Tribu-lation Kingdom on earth
First Coming	Pente-cost	End of Acts	2nd Cominge
Israel and the people of God Israel in the land Israel is first Temple, ceremonies Visible organiaation The 12 Apostles of Israel The Kingdom is near Miracles, powers, signs Visible intervention of angels Prophecies accomplished		Israel rejected Israel dispersed No distinction Temple destroyed. Nothing visible Invisible organism Paul All blessings in above-heavens Faith only Silence of God Hidden till now in God	Same as during Acts

It would be difficult for us to comprehend fully the impact produced on Christians by the setting aside of Israel. It was evidently a grave crisis for everything seemed to collapse. From first-century documents we learn that a majority of believers presumed that Israel had definitively ceased to be the elected people and was now replaced by a Church composed mainly of Christian Gentiles forming a visible organization; all the promises made to Israel would now be realized spiritually within this Church.

But in spite of this catastrophe and a break in the "normal" manner of accomplishing the Divine plan, humanity is not abandoned. God has not only opened a sphere of heavenly blessings during Acts (to provoke Israel to jealousy), but now He reveals to Paul that which had been hidden for all time and from all generations: an economy, or dispensation, which mirrors the final state where God will be all in all. The believer has access to all spiritual blessings in the "above heavens",[111] at the right hand of God (Eph. 1:20; 2:6), in Christ Jesus. Whereas some degree of communion with the Lord was possible during Acts, in his last Epistles written after Acts, Paul speaks of a complete communion where Christ is our life and lives in our hearts.

Our work *The Teachings of the Apostle Paul* is a detailed examination of all that relates to this new dispensation of grace. There is mentioned there "unsearchable riches," Eph. 3:8, which far exceed all that we could obtain by limiting ourselves to blessings offered Israel, and which more than compensate all that we may appear to be losing by giving up the idea that our Church has replaced Israel, ceremonies included.

We skip over the whole period which follows the time of Acts – during which Israel is not the people of God – to review the time which precedes the Kingdom on earth. On our sketch above, we have indicated that this future time will have the same characteristics as the time of Acts, because, once more, the Kingdom is near and the prophecies will be accomplished.[112]

The period in which we now live thus constitutes a complete interruption in the 'normal' accomplishment of God's purposes. It completely escapes the vision of the prophets.[113] The national restoration – preceding the religious restoration – as well as other current events, may be looked upon as a *preparation* for the realization of certain prophecies, but not yet their accomplishment itself.

During the times of the Gospels and Acts this interruption was not yet known, because Israel's repentance could have been expected to occur at any time. The Gospels and the Epistles written during the time of Acts therefore present the events of the end, and the coming of the Lord as if it were to follow those times without interruption. (See, e.g.: Matt. 24; Acts 3; 1 & 2 Thess.) In those times, just as during the end of the present age, expectation of the imminent coming of the Lord was justified.

The unexpected, radical change which occurred at the end of Acts should make us wary in applying to ourselves that which was valid during earlier times, especially where organizations and ceremonies are concerned, i.e. with all visible things in general.

h. The End Times of the Present Age

Towards the end of the present age, the 5th kingdom of Daniel's prophecy, Dan. 2:41-43, will be formed; this is represented by the feet of the great statue, which are made of a mixture of iron and clay. It will be a divided kingdom, grouping 10 powers, represented by the 10 horns of the symbolic animal of Rev. 17, who will attack the Lamb. The advent of this divided kingdom will be one of the signs that the present period is ending and that the prophecies begin anew to be accomplished.

Israel, part of whom have already returned to their land, will again become the people of God, as will be manifested by the restoration of the Temple. Texts such as Matt. 24:15; 2 Thess. 2:4, and Rev. 11:1, 2, which refer to these end times do indeed speak of this Temple.

Signs of the end times of our age are summarized by the Lord Himself in Matt. 24. First, He warns against drawing too hasty conclusions that the end itself might be imminent. There will be many false Christs,[114] wars, famines, and earthquakes – but all this will only be the beginning of sorrows. The Jews will be persecuted, iniquity will increase, the charity of most will cool off, but, nevertheless the good news of the Kingdom will be proclaimed in the whole world.

The most dramatic period will come when Israel will see the "abomination of desolation" established in the Holy place. The Lord here refers to the prophet Daniel and advises: "who readeth, let him understand," Matt. 24:15. This prophet does refer, several times, to an individual represented symbolically by the "little horn" of a dreadful beast, Dan. 7:8, 21-25.

Daniel also calls him "a king of fierce countenance," "understanding dark sentences," Dan. 8:23, and "a vile person," Dan. 11:21-30. This individual becomes powerful through mischief, intrigue, deceit, strength. He concludes an alliance with Israel during the seventy weeks of years determined upon Israel, Dan. 9:24-27, but ends the sacrifice and the oblation after 3 1/2 years, Dan. 8:11-13; 9:27; 11:31; 12:11, and the abomination of desolation is then set up in the Temple, Dan. 8:13; 9:27; 11:31; 12:11; Matt. 24:15; 2 Thess. 2:3, 4. In that time begins the great tribulation, such as never had been since the beginning of the cosmos, Matt. 24:21; Dan. 12:1. The false prophets performing great signs and wonders will be particularly dangerous, "insomuch that, if it were possible, they shall deceive the very elect," Matt. 24:24.

The person spoken of especially by Daniel already had a forerunner in his time, Antioch Epiphanus, and there had been several others after him. But none of them accomplished what the Scriptures say about this "fierce king." He appears to fit the description of the person who Paul calls "the man of sin, the son of perdition; who opposeth and exalteth himself above all that is called God or that is worshipped; so that he as God sitteth in the temple of God shewing himself that he is God.", 2 Thess. 2:3, 4.[115]

He also appears to be represented by the first "beast" of Rev. 13. The second beast in these texts, i.e. the false prophet of Rev. 16:3, 19:20, and 20:10 would then correspond to the person John calls the antichrist, 1 John 2:18, 22; 4:3; 2 John 7.

As a representative worthy of Satan, he is also **the** liar, pre-eminently. He denies that Jesus is the Christ, the Son of God, and opposes the Truth, i.e. the Word of God, by any and all means.

Revelation provides us with much information about this time which precedes the Kingdom,[116] where Satan desperately exerts himself to defeat the posterity of the woman, destroy Israel, and set up his throne at the place where the Lord will have His throne. (Rev. 2:13; 13:2; 16:10.) Babylon, the ancient gathering site of satanic opposition, seems to have to be rebuilt in that time, for we read, in Rev. 18:19, that that city will be completely destroyed in one hour.[117]

The disasters at the end of this age will culminate in a great final battle by the kings "of all the earth" who will be gathered in the place called, in Hebrew, Harmaguedon, Rev. 16:16. This is, most likely, the valley of Megiddo where all the great battles of the Middle East have taken place. Joel 3:2, 12 and Zech. 14:2 tell us that all the nations will also assemble in the valley of Jehoshaphat, near Jerusalem, and will attack that city. That is where the nations will be judged by the Lord.

There are many references in the OT to: "The day of the Lord" (or "for the Lord").[118] It is a day or a time of judgment when the Lord exhibits His power. Isa. 2:12, 17 summarizes the characteristics of that day: "For the day of the Lord of hosts shall be upon everyone that is proud and lofty, and upon everyone that is lifted up; and he shall be brought low... and the Lord alone shall be exalted in that day." But the day of the Lord pre-eminently will be the last day (of 24 hours) of our present age, that "great and notable day of the Lord" mentioned in Acts 2:20 which is a quotation of Joel 2:31. It will be a day of utter darkness[119] which will end the 3 1/2 years. There will also be "a great earthquake, such as was not since men were upon the earth, so mighty an earthquake, and so great." (Rev. 16, 19; also Isa. 13:13; 34:4; Joel 3:16; Zech. 14:4; Rev. 6:14; 11:13.) And there will be other cosmic phenomena. It is then that the two witnesses of Rev. 11:12 will ascend up to heaven and that "the times of the nations" will end (Luke 21:24 and see Note 21 in Section IVb. The Law and the Old Covenant).

In all these events, it is always Israel that is especially kept in view, and it is through the great tribulation that this people will finally be led to say: "Blessed is He Who comes in the name of the Lord" and to be converted. (Zech. 12:1-14; 13:8, 9; Mal. 3:3, 4.) When the Lord's disciples will see all those things happening during those last years of the age, they will know that the Son of man is near, at the door, Matt. 24:33, and they will therefore have to watch and be ready because they will not know at what day, what hour, their Lord will come, Matt. 24:42, 44.

It is also during the day of the Lord that the resurrection out of the dead of regenerated[120] and justified[121] men will occur. And those still living at that time will undergo a transformation such that they will never die, John 11:26, and even receive a spiritual body which is not subject to the natural laws to which we are accustomed, and which will permit them to be caught up to meet the Lord in the air, together with those resurrected ones with bodies having the same properties, 1 Cor. 15:51, 52; 1 Thess. 4:17.[122]

At the sound of the last trumpet (Isa. 27:13; Joel 2:1, 15; Zeph. 1:16; Matt. 24:31; 1 Cor. 15:52; 1 Thess. 4:15; Rev. 10:7; 11:15), the Son of man will come from heaven with power and great glory, Matt. 24:30, with all the angels, Matt. 24:31; 1 Thess. 3:13; 2 Thess. 1:7. And it is on the mount of Olives that the Lord's feet shall stand, as Zech. 14:4 informs us, and this mount will be split in two, so forming a valley between them.

At this glorious appearing of the Lord the Kingdom of the world will be committed to Him, and He will take up His great power and take possession of His reign on earth, Rev. 11:15, 17; 12:10; 16:1, 6.

The "beast" and the "false prophet" are cast into the lake of fire, Rev. 19:20, Satan is bound for a thousand years and cast into the bottomless pit, Rev. 20:1-3.

So ends the "present evil age" of Gal. 1:4.

THE AGE TO COME

The Son of man is sitting on the throne of glory (Matt. 19:28; 25:31) and the 12 Apostles are similarly sitting on 12 thrones, judging the 12 tribes of Israel. It is the "renewing of all things" (Matt. 19:28), or the new birth of the world.[123] The restoration is in good hands, it is the time of "the restitution of all things"[124] of which God spoke in times past through the mouth of his holy prophets. Abraham is resurrected, and the promises made to him by the Lord can now be realized. He comes into possession of "all the land of Canaan" during the entire age (Gen. 17:8, where "everlasting" indicates the duration of this age), and all the families of the earth are blessed in him.

All this concerns the earthly sphere. But Abraham is also "heir of the world" (Rom. 4:13), which includes the earth and the heavens; together with him is his posterity blessed.

In the preceding chapters we have reviewed briefly what the Prophets have to say about the restoration of Israel to their land. We have seen the beginning of the realization of all those promises in the Gospels and in Acts. But it is in this age to come that the promises are finally accomplished: Israel is no longer divided, as formerly, but now constitute a visible unity on earth (see, for example, Jer. 3:18; 31:1; 50:4; 5, 20; Eze. 37:15-28). This unity will be centred around a King before Whom all the nations shall bow.[125] He will be praised by all;[126] David will reign.[127]

Creation will be delivered from the bondage of corruption and participate in "the glorious liberty of the children of God," Rom. 8:21. One recalls the ancient promises: "the land shall yield her increase, and the trees of the field shall yield their fruit. And your threshing shall reach unto the vintage, and the vintage shall reach into the sowing time...", Lev. 26:4, 5. Since Israel will obey and practice the Commandments, all this will be realized. And so will be the visions of the Prophets: "The pastures are clothed with flocks; the valleys also are covered over the corn." (Ps. 65:13; Isa. 30:23-25; 49:10; Jer. 31:4, 5, 12-14; Zech. 3:10; Amos 9:13, 14). "The wilderness and the solitary place shall be glad... the desert shall rejoice, and blossom as the rose" (Isa. 32:15; 35:1, 2; 43:19, 20; Eze.

34:26, 27; 36:33-36). "The wolf also shall dwell with the lamb..." (Isa. 11:6-8; 35:9).

It will be an era of justice and peace (Ps. 72:1-4; 85:11-14; Isa. 2:1-4; 11:9; 32:16, 17; 60:17; Jer. 23:5; Mic. 4:1, 11), while all efforts in this present evil age will fail because man wants to establish peace by his own efforts, without the Lord.

We have already mentioned the fact that the length of life will be increased, probably to the same extent as that in the second age, Isa. 65:20; Ps. 92:13-15. Israel will increase[128], will reach the new birth and receive the spiritual power from on high[129] because her iniquity will be forgiven.[130]

We have previously seen that in that age the Law must still be observed,[131] but it will now be written in the hearts of the Jews, and they will observe it, not by their own power, but by the power of the Spirit. The New Covenant will replace the Old Covenant. Israel will be "a kingdom of priests[132] and thus the earth will be full of the knowledge of the Lord (Isa. 11:9; 29:24). There will be shepherds according to the heart of the Lord (Jer. 3:15), under the Good Shepherd (Isa. 40:11; Eze. 34:12-16, 22-24; Ps. 23), the Great Shepherd (Heb. 13:20), the Chief Shepherd (1 Pet. 5:4).

Israel will be pre-eminent and be served by the other nations,[133] not in its own interest but to be a blessing to others;[134] Matt. 28:19 will then be realized. Evangelization will be accompanied by the power proper to that age, Heb. 6:5.

Then, and then only, will we see a visible Church on earth with a visible Head, that which the Lord had promised to build, Matt. 16:18.

After the 1000 years Satan is released for a short time (Rev. 20:3, 7), and he deceives the nations (Eze. 38:8-12; 39:12-16) and incites them to attack Jerusalem. But a fire which comes down from heaven devours him, and the devil is cast into the lake of fire and brimstone.[135] Then comes the judgment before the Great White Throne of all those who have not yet taken part in one of the previous resurrections.

God has reached a first goal: the new birth, not only of men but of the whole earth. That which Adam should have done has now been accomplished by the Son. A witness has been given to spiritual creatures: He has put all enemies under the feet of the Son, 1 Cor. 15:25.

Nearly all that we have summarized above relates to the earth. But it is understood that those who belong to the heavenly sphere are not inactive. On the contrary, Abraham and all those who are blessed with him, Gal. 3:9, and who have arrived at the justification by faith in Jesus Christ carry out their functions by intervening in the earthly sphere. Their actions are manifested by miracles, signs, and powerful actions which were foreshadowed in the times of the Gospels and Acts, Heb. 6:5. The angels too, practice a visible ministry in favor of those who shall be heirs of salvation, Heb. 1:14.

Finally, during this age and the one which follows, those who have been placed at the right hand of God in the above-heavenly sphere show the exceeding riches of the grace of God, Eph. 2:7. Since they are united with the Lord Jesus Christ as intimately as is possible, they participate in all these activities.

During the coming age, we thus see three groups, each forming a unity, which are at different states or degrees of communion with the Lord: on earth, Israel; in the heavens, the "sons" blessed with Abraham; in the above-heavens, those who have reached "the measure of the status of the fulness of Christ," Eph. 4:13. All are regenerated, and in this sense constitute one group, but they have reached different stages along the way of salvation. The "sons" have already reached the sphere of blessings of the fifth age, while those who are sitting at the right hand of God already partake, in spirit, of the perfect state where God will be all in all. We see a correlation between the "vertical" distinctions (position) and the "horizontal" distinctions (according to the ages).

Individually, believers may progress anytime from one sphere to the next one[136], but the great masses will proceed through the eons before reaching the final goal purposed by God.

THE NEW CREATION

The fifth age is called "the day of God," and in view of its coming, "the heavens being on fire shall be dissolved, and the elements shall melt with fervent heat," 2 Pet. 3:10-12. Neither the earth nor the heavens will be annihilated, but they will be changed. Thus the Apostle follows up these verses with: "nevertheless we, according to His promise, look for new heavens and a new earth..." This corresponds to the visions of the Apostle John: "And I saw a new heaven and a new earth".[137] Since John just finished speaking about "a lake of fire" at the end of the coming age, (the 4th), we are inclined to equate this with the general conflagration spoken of by Peter. Who shall escape it? Only those whose bodies are immune to fire, those who, after having shared the death with Christ, are justified and have received a new body either while still living or at resurrection. They will then have a spiritual body with properties differing from those we know today. That new body will not be affected by fire, just as was the case when the Lord walked with Daniel's three friends in Nebuchadnezzar's fiery furnace, Dan. 3:25.

All those living in the 5th age will therefore have passed through the new birth and have become "sons of God;" these belong to the heavenly sphere. The latter now extends over the earth and absorbs the earthly sphere. We read, indeed, that the "New Jerusalem" which had always been above (Gal. 4:26), which is "heavenly" (Heb. 11:16; 12:22; 2 Cor. 5:1), comes down out of heaven (Rev. 21:2). The inspired authors necessarily had to use words with which we are familiar and which designate things of our current age in order to describe the splendor of that city. Since all those things of the 5th age will be completely different from those we know today, it is evident that the reality of those things escapes us completely. Here we encounter the same powerlessness in trying to know those things that we have already encountered in descriptions of the 1st age, when Isaiah and Ezekiel were trying to describe to us the "covering cherub" who after his fall, was named Satan. The 2nd and 4th ages are more or less comprehensible to us, the 1st and 5th escape us entirely; to understand them would be to bring them down to our level.

However, the Apostle tries to give us a rough impression of the state of things. First, he can tell us what there will not be: sea, sufferings, night and day, death, Temple, curse, sin.[138] Then he follows this with a few generalizations: God "dwells" with men, the glory of God lights up the "city" (which explains why there is no day or night). These indications enable us to perceive that he is talking about an inexpressible glory which surpasses, not in degree but in nature, the already magnificent state of the 4th age.

In this 5th age we see a state which corresponds to that of primitive creation (1st age), which was good and where sin had not yet appeared. But the absence of sin in the 5th age does not mean that all is as perfect as God Himself. Thus we see that there is still a "tree of life," the leaves of which are for the "healing" of the nations. The absence of death, of crying, of pain, of sorrow, show that there is no question of medical healing, but of help or "assistance" in order to attain the full measure of glory which is obtainable in that age.[139]

During the 4th age, the Lord Jesus Christ reigns; at the end of that age all that is sinful is destroyed all rule, all authority and all enemy power are put down, 1 Cor. 15:24, 25. Verse 25 shows that "rule, authority and power" are not used in an absolute sense, but of all that is *enemy*. Thus, Rev. 22:5 shows that some are still reigning" during the 5th age. Death itself has been swallowed up in victory when all have arrived at incorruptibility: there is no death in this age, Rev. 21:4. All else has been consumed by fire. After the 4th age the Lord will not cease to reign,[140] but will deliver the Kingdom to God (1 Cor. 15:24). During the 5th age there is indeed mention of "the throne of God and of the Lamb" (Rev. 22:1, 3). The Lord, therefore, reigns with the Father.

GOD ALL IN ALL

In all other publications[141] we examine in greater detail all that which deals with reconciliation, which is expressed by the Greek words "katallasso" and "apokatallasso." The first degree represents the ending of the "enemy attitude" that God had to take towards the sinful creature. God is reconciled through the death of His Son, regardless of the attitude of men. The throne of God is a throne of grace; in fact, His love is free to act in Justice because the Son died for sins. Reconciliation is for all, but all do not accept it. To obtain reconciliation one must, through Christ, be in communion with Him, die with Him, and thereby take part in the punishment which must befall the sinner to satisfy justice. Being dead to sin, one is justified.

But all this remains in the earthly sphere. Paul revealed later that there is more: that a closer communion with Christ can bring the creature to be placed at the right hand of God, outside of creation, in the sphere of perfection. And that is when Paul uses the word "apokatallasso." It is no longer the "katallasso" accepted by man, but a complete reconciliation which comes from God, which arises out of the possible identification of the believer with the glorified Jesus Christ. As we have seen, this is God's final goal: God all in all, 1 Cor. 15:28. In his Epistle to the Colossians Paul says: "...by Him to reconcile (apokatallaxai) all things unto Himself".[142] **That** is the will of God. He has prepared everything: not only the katallasso but also the apokatallasso. He wishes that we accept both (2 Cor. 5:20) and that His creatures thus progress from glory to glory, in complete freedom.

When God will be all in all, He will have reached His goal and achieved the impossible: He will have increased His glory by creating and perfecting His creature. Being all in all, there is consequently no more Mediator, no King, no Priest; the Son has been all these but has now completed His Work. He Himself now has the glory that was His before His humiliation, and He has elevated the creature with Him. Freedom, that supreme gift, was about to be lost by the creature who was misusing it; but now it is complete because the creature has freely decided to completely align its will with the will of God. Where only one will exists, freedom is perfect because there is no longer any evil to which one might be subjected. As long as two separate beings exist, freedom might be endangered because division might occur; but when perfection has been reached, when God is all in all, the partial, the relative, do not exist any more. Unity, however, does not abolish individuality, multiplicity, personality. But all those individualities will have the same mind, the same thoughts, the same spirit (Phil. 2:2; Eph. 4:3, 13), will understand each other completely, and form a glorious unity.

CONCLUSION

Referring to our statements in the Introduction, we trust that we have demonstrated that a "scientific" approach to the study of the Scriptures – without preconceived ideas and with an attitude of mind which searches above all for the complete truth, giving up any personal conviction which is not supported by the written Word – may lead to an understanding of the Divine plan which harmonizes all the inspired information given to us.

The reader may have realized that by so proceeding, one avoids many theological problems – created by unjustified *a prioris* – the solution of which have always contributed to divide Christendom. Further, the apparent contradictions and imperfections which lead to destructive criticism are eliminated. This is the only method which could produce, in collaboration with everybody, a unique science of the Scriptures, always capable of being perfected, and expressing more accurately the integral Truth.

This, of course, does not mean a purely intellectual study, for the goal must be to come to a better knowledge of Jesus Christ, of Whom the whole written Word speaks, to better love Him and to praise the glory of the grace of God which He bestowed on us through His Son.

It is quite possible that some of the conclusions which we have come to draw conflict with those of the reader. We deeply regret this and beg him to understand that we too may have shared some of those opinions, but that an objective study compelled us to abandon them. We invite the reader to examine anew those questions, applying the "scientific" method, thus by not starting off with preconceived ideas. Far from pretending that we ourselves have reached the complete Truth, we would be grateful to be able to correct our ideas. But the friendly reader who would be inclined to correct us should not limit himself to a criticism of certain details or certain consequences resulting from our "system" basing himself on his own "system," or merely present a particular point of view with which we are probably already acquainted; he should try to present a "system," if you will, which better explains all that the Scriptures wish to teach us.

After we have come to some understanding of the Divine plan in general, we must examine in greater detail the characteristics of the present time and also that which concerns the various spheres of blessings; then we must find out how all this concerns us personally. This we have attempted in our works: *The Teachings of the Apostle Paul* and *The Way of Salvation.*

APPENDIX 1: ETERNITY

In most cases, the word "eternity" is the translation of the Hebrew word "olam" or of the Greek word "aion." Usually, it is clear that these words do not indicate an unlimited period of time; but there are cases where it might be thought that they refer to something that we call "eternity," a period which has no end, a time which continues without limits. There is much to be said about this, but we will confine ourselves to a brief examination to determine whether the Scriptures do speak of a time without end.

First of all, it must be observed that the idea of time is only secondary in "olam" and "aion." The plural of olam (olamim) is used twelve times in the O.T., (for instance in 1 Kings 8:13, "for ever;" Ps. 145:13, "everlasting;" Eccl. 1:10, "of old time"). Similarly, the N.T. uses the plural of aion (aiones). Scripture speaks about various olamim and aiones, which each have their own characteristics and duration. Thus Luke 20:34, 35 establishes a contrast between "this" world (aion) and "that" world (the aion to come). And in 1 Chron. 16:36 and other texts we read: "for ever and ever," and this expression must be taken literally, i.e. from olam to olam, (according to the Hebrew text).

The expression "olam va ed," which means "during the age and after" is, typically, translated "for ever and ever." Ps. 119:44 and other texts show that, here also, we must accept the expression literally.

Eph. 2:7 speaks of the ages to come; there are therefore more than one which are yet to come. And Eccl. 1:10 mentions some olamim which preceded us. By examining all the texts in the inspired language, and by distinguishing the different "worlds," "days," and "heavens," we are led to recognize five eons, or ages. These eons are defined by major events. The sketch below illustrates the results of an investigation relating to the ages, results which harmonize with all that the Scriptures say on this subject, and which confirm what we can discover by a straight-forward examination of the purposes of God.

There remains to be seen whether there might be certain expressions in the Bible that indicate an unlimited period of time. The main argument in support of this view is that Scripture speaks of an "everlasting God" (tou aioniou theou), Rom. 16:26. Now, the fact that God is, and that He is not limited by time, cannot be expressed by a word appropriate to the periods pertaining to that which was created. Even if supposing that "aionios" or other expressions such as "world without end" did indicate an unlimited time, a succession of periods without end this would not adequately characterize God: time is a notion relating to creation, and God **is** before and after time. There is a Divine "eternal" (outside of time) which has nothing whatever in common with what man can imagine in relation to time. The expression "Eternal God," i.e., "God of the ages," says nothing about the nature of God, but simply expresses the fact that the eons were created by Him (Heb. 1:2), and that He continually acts during these eons to bring the creature back to Him.

All the expressions in the original text which use the words olam or aion must be taken literally. Thus, Rom. 16:27 says: "unto the eons of eons" and indicates thereby the last two eons, the pre-eminent eons, just as "holy of holies" indicates the holy place, pre-eminently.

If one should take exception to the idea that "eternal" life is limited, we would first reply that it is at least limited by a beginning. Then we can point to Mark 10:30, for instance, which clearly speaks of a life to be lived in the age to come. Here again, "eternal" does not emphasize the length but the *type* of life. It is a real life where the body itself is quickened by an action of the Spirit. This life will last throughout the age, not to cease at the end but to be elevated to a higher sphere until the perfect state is reached by an identification with Christ: God all in all. The 'eternal' life is then terminated, to be changed into perfect life in God.

THE TIMES OF THE AGES (EONS)

(The Ages were prepared by God, Heb.1:2)

BEFORE THE AGES — 1Cor.2:7

AFTER THE AGES

GOD ALL IN ALL
1Cor.15:28
Fulness of times Eph.1:10
Complete Reconciliation. (apokatallasso) Eph.2:16

GOD "is"
John 1:1
1Cor.2:7
2Tim.1:9
Tit.1:2

The world that then was. 2Pet.3:6
The world that is now, 2Pet.3:7
The world to come. The Day of God, 2Pet.3:12

1	2	3	4	5
Original Creation	Kingdom planned (Eons prepared anew, (note 1))	Present Age (Separation)	Kingdom established Isa 65:17 (note 2)	New Creation Rev.21:1

Creation Gen.1:1
Overthrow (katabole) & Restoration Gen.1:2
The Flood Gen.8 & 9
Second Coming
Purification by fire (2Pet.3:7)

The Ages which were before us Eccl.1:10
The present evil Age Gal.1:4
The Age Which is to come (Eph.1:21)
The Age of Ages (Eph.3:21)
The Ages to come (Eph.2:7)

The Lord's Day (Rev.1:10)
The day of the Lord (Joel 1:15; Acts 2:20; 2Pet.3:10)

Note 1. Heb 11:3: "The eons were prepared anew" (katartizo). The word "katartizo" has the special sense of "perfecting by preparing" or "preparing anew." (See also CB Appendix 125.8)

Note 2. Conditions on earth are as in the days of Noah, Age No. 2. (Isa 65:20; Ps 92:12-14)

The Divine Plan and its realization   97

So we see that a clear understanding of the eons broadens our ideas and, far from losing anything, shows us a life better than "eternal" life, than the life which relates to the eons, to creation, and which has not yet reached absolute perfection. The Epistles to Ephesians, Philippians, and Colossians already open today the way to that perfect state.

Some have believed to glorify the Lord by saying that He is the "eternal" King, the "eternal" Priest, the "eternal" Redeemer, etc., meaning thereby that He will never cease to be all these things – which really implies that He will never reach the final goal: God all in all. On the contrary, He must one day cease to be King, Priest, Redeemer, etc. because His Work will have been accomplished. That which is "eternal," which relates to the eons, is still under sin or imperfection. After the eons have ended, the need for that which is "eternal" no longer exists because absolute perfection will have been reached. Similarly, an "eternal" covenant in the sense of a covenant without end would permanently maintain an imperfect state where two parties would still exist. Any covenant must end when its purpose has been accomplished. At the end of the eons, there can be no question of a covenant because absolute unity in God will have been attained.

A detailed study on this subject has been made by Mr. G.J. Puptit in his book written in Dutch, *De Tijden der Eeuwen*, (the Times of the Ages).

APPENDIX 2: THE HUMAN BODY

It is generally assumed that our body consists solely of the material part of our being, while soul and spirit are spiritual and can leave the body. In this sphere also it will be necessary to review and correct our ideas to render them more Scriptural. Many pagan notions have sneaked in, to be reshaped later by tradition. Unfortunately, it has become difficult to escape their influence. We cannot examine all these questions here, but we will attempt to more accurately define the scriptural notion of the human "body."

If the body were solely material, it would disappear after death and the molecules and inherent forces would be assimilated by other organisms. Resurrection of the body would then be impossible, because this would lead to absurdities which have led some to completely reject the idea of resurrection[143]. This is one of the cases where believers have contributed, by their non-scriptural affirmations, to bring about the present state of confusion, agnosticism, and atheism.

Scripture tells us that the body subsists, not only for those whose bodies will be changed at the coming of the Lord, but also for those who have died. Let us look at the following texts, for example:

> Rom. 8:11. "shall also quicken your mortal bodies;"
> Rom. 8:23. "the redemption of our body;"
> 1 Cor. 15:42-44. "It (the body) is sown in corruption; it is raised in incorruption; it is sown in dishonor, it is raised in glory; it is sown in weakness, it is raised in power. It is sown a natural body; it is raised a spiritual body."
> 1 Cor. 15:52. "we shall be changed."
> 1 Cor. 15:53. "For this corruptible must put on incorruption, and this mortal must put on immortality..."
> Phil. 3:21. "Who shall change our vile body, that it may be fashioned like unto His glorious body."

These texts make it clear that the word "body" frequently implies more than the idea of matter. After resurrection one still possesses one's body,[144] but it will be incorruptible and glorious, powerful, spiritual, immortal. And note that the Word does not say that we will receive a new body, but rather, that it uses expressions such as: "quicken your body," "redemption," "resurrection," "put on," "change," "transform." The body, therefore remains but has a different form of existence. The body is an organism which is not material in itself, but which can present itself to our senses as being made up of molecules; the latter are incidental, they are not the essential. Other molecules may replace the former molecules without in any way changing the body in its essence. Best of all, at resurrection the body takes on a new form of existence which surpasses our present "natural" state and is thus incomprehensible to us; if there are going to be molecules, they will not have the characteristics of what we call "matter."

What happens after death? The spirit of life no longer operates on the organism, cell life ceases, organic molecules decompose. The body remains but the incidental, i.e. that which is material, disappears. This is what Paul calls being "naked" (2 Cor. 5:3), "unclothed," v. 4. In this passage Paul distinguishes three states:

1. By "this tabernacle" he means the material state, our usual state.
2. By "our house which is from heaven," the spiritual state after resurrection.
3. By "naked" or "unclothed," the state after death. In verse 4 he expresses the desire to be changed directly from state 1 to state 2, to not go through death, but to be changed (1 Cor. 15:51).

It is important here to realize that the word "body" is used with different meanings and may very well, in everyday language, designate that which is visible, material. Thus, when the Apostle says: "at home in the body" (2 Cor. 5:6), and "willing rather to be absent from the body" (v. 8), he means the body in its present form, the flesh, that which is visible, and not the body in its essence. (See also 2 Cor. 12:2, 3 and Heb. 13:3).

When a man dies he goes to the "Hades," i.e. to the imperceptible. It is the whole man who goes, body included. The body is subject to "natural" laws only in its 'natural' form but not in the "naked" state during death, nor in its glorious state after resurrection.

It is interesting to note that modern biology has been brought to accept ideas corresponding to this concept of a body of non-material essence.

For a while biology was frankly materialistic: the body consisted of matter upon which acted physical forces. Those who dared to speak about a certain non-material "vitality" were looked upon as "obscurantists." Presently, many scientists are coming back to a certain "vitalism" because they cannot otherwise arrive at an explanation for many facts. Thus radiolaria, in the beginning, are formed only from a mass of transparent and shapeless protoplasm containing a nucleus. Later on, needles and concentric envelopes take on a well-defined characteristic shape.

In general, the more or less complicated organisms originate from a single, unstructured cell. Cells produced from successive divisions may be used to form any part of the organism. Often accepted is the idea that it is an immaterial agent which forces the cells to group themselves in accordance with a pre-established plan. In a way, it is this "plan" which constitutes the body.

APPENDIX 3: THE GIANTS

Original Bible texts frequently open up a new world to the researcher. We will not criticize the versions which, as the product of human endeavor, are excellent. If one accepts the verbal inspiration of the Scriptures, it must also be admitted that no man will be able to interpret this Divine document perfectly. Here too, we must learn to recognize the inferior position of man as well as the need for continually referring to God. It might be thought that in order to obtain a more accurate knowledge of the inspired text than the translators provided us with, we would need to be more learned than they were. Their translations are generally good, and in most cases it will suffice to examine certain words more closely – and this can be done by any believer willing to do so. All that is needed is: 1) one's sanctified intelligence, and 2) a good concordance which lists all the original words and references to all the texts where these words are used. As a suggestion, the following might be consulted: *Englishman's Greek Concordance of the New Testament* and *Englishman's Hebrew and Chaldee Concordance of the Old Testament*. Other help may be useful, but one must never accept the affirmations of human documents without verification, and this applies to the best dictionaries, commentaries, etc. Only the Word gives the decisive signification, and any believer is in a position to be able to judge as well or better than the greatest scholar. The work of the scholar should be primarily directed to facilitating the personal search of others; he should not impose his conclusions upon others.

After these general comments, let us examine what the Bible teaches us about the giants.

Let us take a closer look at the dwellers in Canaan.[145] They occupied the land promised to Abraham and Israel (Gen. 12:6). There, we find, for example, the Rephaims (Gen. 14:5; 1 Chron. 20:4), the Zuzims or Zamzummims (Gen. 14:5; Deut. 2:20), the Emims (Gen. 14:5; Deut. 2:10), the Horites (Gen. 14:6; 36:20; Deut. 2:12), the Kenites (Gen. 15:19; Judges 4:11), etc.

The Rephaim, particularly, have drawn the attention of archeologists and of those who study the Bible.[146] The name is derived from Rapha, their father. In Hebrew, the corresponding verb signifies "healing." They were, very likely, the first "healers," and practiced occultism. The Greeks translated Rephaim by Katachlonioi, designating thereby "spirits" of the dead which were supposed to influence nature in general and the climate in particular. A Phoenician inscription on the sarcophagus of the king Tabmit Z 8 of Sidon refers to such spirits.

The Bible names several children of Rapha, who are very tall or monstrous one way or another[147]:

> Og, the king of Basham, with his bedstead of iron (Deut. 3:11);
> Goliath of Gath, of very tall stature (1 Sam. 17:4);
> Lahmi, a brother of Goliath, with the huge spear (2 Sam. 21:19; 1 Chron. 20:5);'Ishbi-benob, with the heavy spear (2 Sam. 21:16);
> Saph (2 Sam. 21:18);
> Sippai (1 Chron. 20:4);
> The man of great stature, with six fingers and six toes (1 Sam. 21:20).

The Emims and Zanzumims are also of great stature and of the family of the Rephaim (Deut. 2:11, 20).

Let us now turn to the Anakims. They were also tall (Deut. 2:10, 21) and are named after Anak, whose father is Arba (Josh. 14:15; 15:13). The three sons of Anak are named: Ahiman, Sheshai, and Talmai (Num. 13:22; Josh, 15:14). Who were those Anakims? They are not named – no more than are the other races of which we are speaking here – among the children of Shem, Ham or Japheth. Num. 13:33 gives us an indication:

> "And there we saw the nephilim (and) the sons of Anak, which come of the giants (nephilim)."

We must therefore find out who are those Nephilim. The word seems to be closely related to the verb "naphal" (to fall). They are first mentioned in Gen. 6:4:

> "There were Nephilim (Hebrew text) in the earth in those days; and also after that."

We read in Gen. 6 that the "sons of God" took the daughters of Adam for wives, and Gen. 6:4 shows that the Nephilim came from these unions. Let us look a step further and see who were those "sons of God."

The Hebrew text reads "sons of Elohim," an expression which is never used to designate men,[148] but is always applied to angels.[149] We must then place ourselves from the point of view of those to whom these words were addressed in the first place. It is certain that the Jews who were reading Gen. 6:4 could not interpret "sons of Elohim" by anything other than angels. This is also confirmed by the *Book of Enoch* to which Jude 14 refers and which, therefore, deserves our consideration. Jude 6 and 7 tells us about angels "which kept not their first estate," who "left their own habitation." The Greek word for "habitation" is the same word which is translated "house" in 2 Cor. 5:2 and refers to the heavenly sphere. (The words "vice against nature" is the translation of an expression which literally says: "to come to different flesh.")

From the preceding, combined with Gen.6:2, it results that those "sons of Elohim" were fallen angels which had not kept their first estate, who left (or were expulsed from) the heavenly spheres and took on a fleshly form to unite with the different flesh of the daughters of Adam. The Nephilim were the direct descendants of this union, Gen. 6:4.

It is probably these same angels (or others of the same kind), called "spirits" (as in Ps. 104:4; Heb. 1:7, 14), that are referred to in 1 Pet. 3:19, 20; and 2 Pet. 2:4, 5. These spirits were put "in prison," cast down into hell and delivered into chains of darkness, reserved unto the day of judgment, and the Lord after His resurrection went to them to proclaim His victory. We must note that the word "spirit" is never used to designate a man, except after his resurrection when his body will be governed entirely by the spirit. The dead, besides, are not in prison but in the Hades. In 1 Pet. 3:19 the word "preached" is not the translation of "euangelizo" ("to announce the good news"), but of "kerusso," i.e. to proclaim, as a herald.

The ancient books of the Jews, such as those of the *Jubilees*, the *Maccabees,* of *Sirach, Baruch,* the *Sapiential books*, etc. speak of this judgment of God pronounced on these angels.[150]

On the other hand, it is known that the mythologies speak of "gods" who come down to earth to meet the daughters of men. They, too, speak of heroes who were famous in antiquity (Gen. 6:4). We cannot accept those mythological stories as pure truth, but it seems that they must have been based on historical events described in the Bible. The Babylonian Tablets about creation and the flood, the Egyptian *Book of the Dead*, Greek mythology and other pagan fables may well be a corruption and perversion of primitive truths. We might add that the Arabs and the Koran speak of a race of giants, "Ad" (7:63, 67; 26:123; 41:14; 89:5); they were a proud lot and were exterminated.

A genealogy of the Nephilim, Rephaim, Anakim, and others may be summarized in the form of the sketch below, based on the data given by the Bible:

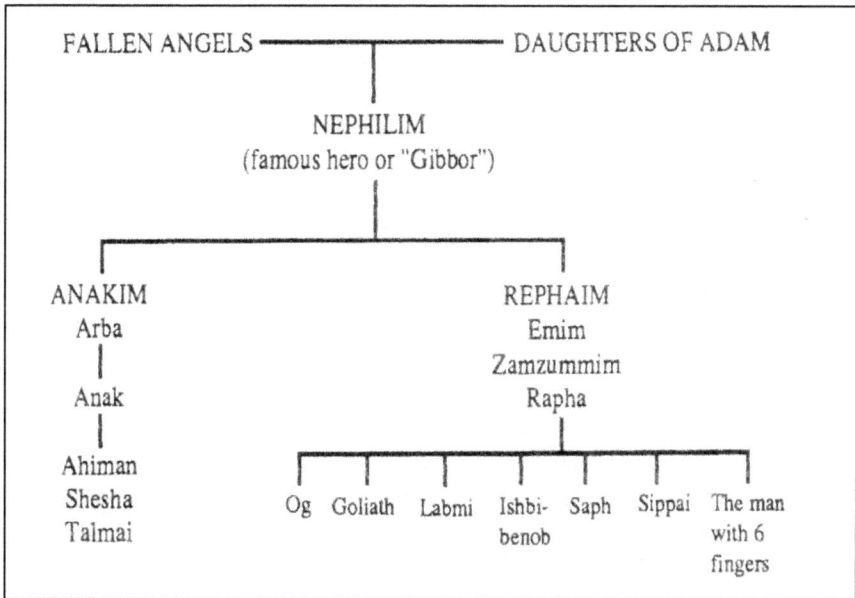

The evil influence exerted by the fallen angels and their progeny on the Adamites, and especially on the Kenites, will have caused, in Mesopotamia, the conditions prevailing before the flood. So we read, in Gen. 6:5:

> "And God saw that the wickedness of man was great in the earth, and that every imagination of the thoughts of his heart was only evil continually.

Evil in this area was suppressed by the flood, but since it did not cover the whole earth, the Nephilim, Anakim, Rephaim, etc. were not all exterminated and remained in various places. That is why Gen. 6:4 tells us that the Nephilim were on the earth also after the flood.

Further notes on the Rephaim

In some versions, the word Rephaim is sometimes translated by "dead," "deceased," or "shadow" particularly in the French versions (*Louis Segond, Darby,* others).

Isa. 26:13-19 is a text difficult to interpret and merits a closer examination. By translating a little more literally, it can be read as follows:

> "…other lords besides thee have dominion over us … dead they shall not live, the Rephaim, (in fact), shall not rise … the earth shall cast out the Rephaim."

This text appears to refer to the influence of diabolic races upon humanity, and gives a contrast between the resurrection of men and the non-resurrection of those beings – whereas the fallen angels (the "spirits" of 1 Pet. 3:19, 20 and 2 Pet. 2:4) are "in prison" until judgment day.

The Rephaim were mighty in size and iniquity, but they were probably not gifted with much intelligence. They could perform extraordinary works, and it is not surprising that the Philistines, the Amorites, and other Canaanite people hired them in their armies or for works requiring great muscular power. The giant city of Bashan, of which Og was the king, and some other monuments made with stones of enormous size may have been built by them.

The famous megalithic monuments are ascribed to them.[151] These, built of huge stones called Dolmen, Cromlech, Menhir, etc. are found in many places but especially in Europe, Africa, and the Near-East. Among the most famous are those of Carnac in Brittany, France.

These monuments are fairly numerous in Palestine, in a region extending from the North-West to the East of the Sea of Galilee. In general, we find many of them in places such as Bashan, Gilead (Deut. 3:1-14), Ammon (Deut. 2:19, 20), the valley of the Rephaim between Jerusalem and

Bethlehem (Josh. 15:8) etc., all places which the Bible mentions in connection with the Rephaim.

Everywhere in the world these monuments are ascribed to the giants, according to tradition.[152] Certain isolated, vertical stones were probably associated with phallic cults. A study of Bible passages containing the word "Asherah," translated in various ways, is instructive. This word is associated with idolatrous cults severely condemned; see for instance Ex. 34:13, Eze. 16:17.

One also recalls the cult of Ashtoreth (the productive [or passive] principle of life) and of Baal (the generative [or active] principle). The "kadesh" (whores and sodomites, Deut. 23:17) were associated with those cults. Finally, the morals of Sodom and Gomorrah must be ascribed to the satanic population living there.

APPENDIX 4: THE FIRST DAY OF THE WEEK

The influence of human tradition is sometimes almost irresistible! Thus we may note the texts where our versions have chosen the translation: "the first day of the week," as follows:

Matt. 28:1	"eis mian sabbaton."
Mark 16:2	"te mia ton sabbaton."
Mark 16:9	"prote sabbatou."
Luke 24:1	"te de mia ton sabbaton."
John 20:1	"te de mia ton sabbaton."
John 20:19	"te emera ekeine te mia sabbaton."
Acts 20:7	"te mia ton sabbaton."
1 Cor. 16:2	"kata mian sabbaton."

Let us first look at the word "mia" (one) translated "first." That which is designated by "one" could also be "first," but not necessarily. Texts such as Matt. 21:19; 26:69; Mark 12:42; etc. even show that it is impossible to write "first." When "first" is to be the meaning, the Greek word "prote" is available.

Second, let us find out if one must add the word "day" which is not found in the Greek text. Grammatically, something must be added because "mia" is feminine and cannot strictly be applied to "sabbaton" which is neuter. Because the word "day" is feminine in Greek and because Matt. 26:17 gives us an example where "day" must be inserted, one may be tempted to do this also in the texts which we are going to examine.

Third, we now come to the word "sabbatôn." No one denies that this is the genitive plural of "sabbaton," but it is generally assumed that it is an idiomatic expression that means "week." One thus translates "first day of the week" whereas it should read: "one (day) of the sabbaths."

It is essential to note the peculiarities of the language, but one must be quite certain that it is impossible, or at least very difficult, to translate literally before translating the Word of God idiomatically. Now, we are not the first to assert that this is not the case here, and we wish to show that a literal translation here is not only natural but indispensable.

The Greek text uses the plural "sabbaton" 26 times, and it seems logical to consult the OT to determine its true meaning. There we find "sabbath" in Hebrew 31 times, and the Septuagint renders it every time in the plural. On the other hand, the word "week" corresponds to the Hebrew "shaboua" which is translated "hebdomas" in the Septuagint. These latter expressions generally have the meaning of "sevens" or a set of seven and are quite distinct from "sabbath" or "shaboua" which means "cessation" (as, for instance, in Gen. 8:22: "day and night shall not cease," confirming the general meaning of "to cease"). A time interval can equally well be defined in terms of a number of weeks as in terms of the same number of sabbaths. One can just as well speak of a feast of "weeks" as of a feast of "sabbaths." But we cannot deduce from this that is always possible to use "week" for "sabbath."

For example, in Lev. 25:8 the sabbaths indicate the years of rest which occurred every 7 years (v. 4). Objectors have pointed to texts such as Luke 18:12 to claim that this obliges us to translate "sabbath" by "week." On the contrary, such a translation deprives the text of its strength. The Pharisee did not fast twice a week, but twice per sabbath, which is to say that he skipped two meals that day. (How "righteous" he must have been!)

When we examine all the OT texts where "sabbath" is used,[153] we come to realize that his expression must be taken literally, that it denotes a series of sabbatical days, either annual feast days or the weekly days of rest. We note particularly the seven sabbaths of Lev. 23:15, 16:

> "And ye shall count unto you from the morrow after the sabbath, from the day that ye brought the sheaf of the wave offering; seven sabbaths shall be complete: Even unto the morrow after the seventh sabbath shall ye number fifty days; and ye shall offer a new meat offering unto the Lord."

There can be no doubt that the literal translation is the correct one, as confirmed by the words "the seventh sabbath." This series of sabbaths *between the Passover and Pentecost* was a unique period of the year.

All this shows therefore that the plural "sabbaths" can have a clearly defined signification, and we would need a strong Scriptural justification before translating the plural "sabbaths" by the singular "week."

But there is more. If all the texts in the NT where our versions read "the first day of the week" all related to the period between the Passover and Pentecost, would it not be obvious that the texts were not referring to any odd sabbath or week, but to the seven sabbaths of Lev. 23? Well, this is precisely what we do find. In the Gospels, this is evident, while for the two other cases where "sabbath" occurs, the context makes it clear for us. In Acts 20:7, the day in question comes after the days of unleavened bread (v. 6) and before Pentecost (v. 16); in 1 Cor. 16:2, the day comes shortly before Pentecost (v. 8).

We can thus be quite certain that one cannot write "the first day of the week." It is, in fact, not about a day of some week or other within the year, but about a particular day in a specific, special period included between the day of the wave offering (after the Passover and Pentecost.[154]

All this also shows that far from replacing the weekly sabbath by a Sunday, Christian Jews in the time of Acts continued to observe the Lord's feasts and all the ceremonies of the Law. After Acts, Paul says explicitly that no one is to be judged in respect of the sabbaths ("sabaton", Col. 2:16).

Sunday is of pagan origin; it is the day of the "sun God" (note: Sontag, Zondag, Dies Dominica, etc.), and its institution has no Scriptural justification. The sabbath will always remain the day of rest during which Israel must do no work, during the periods when they are considered to be the elected people.

For the expression "The day of the Lord," please refer to Chapter IV, section h.

APPENDIX 5:
OBJECTIONS TO THE OBSERVANCE OF THE LAW BY CHRISTIAN JEWS

Rom. 3:21, 28: "without the Law." The Greek word "choris" does not mean "without" in an absolute manner, but rather "apart from." This can be clearly seen by its use in other texts. Thus, for example, Matt. 14:21: "beside women," or better: "apart from the women." In Rom. 3:21 Paul says that he does not abolish the Law but confirms it. To express a total absence, the Greek has "aneu" (without), as in 1 Pet. 4:9.

Rom. 6:14: "ye are not under the law." The Greek text reads "telos," which does not necessarily indicate the end of something, but its outcome; see Matt. 26:58 and Rom. 6:21. The objective of the Law was Christ, it was to bring the Jews to Him. In James 5:11 the Greek text uses the same word when he was speaking of "the end of the Lord." So we see that "the end" by no means indicates a termination; to indicate this, the word "peras" would be used, as in Heb. 6:16.

> Gal. 4:10: "Ye observe…". Verse 9 shows us that his word indicates a wrong manner of observing. They enslaved themselves by trying to observe by their own efforts or as slaves. The Greek word for "to observe" always has a pejorative connotation in Scripture; see Mark 3:2; Acts 9:24 (watched).

Gal. 5:1-11. Paul is still speaking about the "yoke," i.e. about the observation of the Law by their own efforts or as slaves. Circumcision considered as a means in itself and not as an external sign of an internal change is worthless. It is not the Law that justifies, it only gives precepts that we are incapable to follow without grace. Circumcision by itself is worthless, the Law is needed. But all this is not to say that circumcision of the flesh cannot *accompany* the faith. For the Jews, it must be so long as they remain the elected people; it is the sign of the covenant. During the Kingdom on earth, there will be circumcision of the flesh and of the heart, Eze. 44:9.

Heb. 10:18: "No more offering." No more real, effective offering, as that of the Cross: this one has been made once for all. But the symbol may remain, as will be the case during the Kingdom, Eze. 40:40-45. Symbols before the Cross pointed to the future, those after the Cross to the past. There are not any more reasons that they could not exist after the Cross than before. We have already noted that if this passage meant that offerings are suppressed, it should then also be admitted that they had never been demanded. Heb. 10:18 is, indeed, a quotation from the OT (Ps. 40:7-9).

In *The Teachings of the Apostle Paul* we will have the opportunity to examine these questions in greater detail; we will show how the following table may be arrived at:

Standing before God	Standing Before the Law	Standing before sin	Attitude toward the Law	Fulfillment of the Law
1. The non-believer in God	Without Law	Slave to sin	Ignores the Law	Doesn't accomplish the Law
2. Believer in-God but not reborn	"Under" the Law	Slave to sin	Does not delight in Law	Tries to do by himself
3. Believe Jesus is Christ[155]	"In" the Law	Slave to sin	Delights in the Law	Accomplishes the Law partly thru' grace.
4. Believer in Christ-Jesus[156]	Dead to the Law	Delivered from sin	Serves with renewed spirit	The Law is accomplished in him

As an example of 2 above, we have the Jew in general in the OT. During the Kingdom on earth, Jews will be in the position of number 3. Those of the heavenly sphere correspond to number 4. During Acts, the four cases were represented. Those who have died to the Law can still accomplish the Law, but a renewed spirit, thus says Paul at the end of Acts.

APPENDIX 6: ABOUT THE LAST JOURNEY OF PAUL TO JERUSALEM (ACTS 21)

It has been pointed out that the disciples, moved by the Spirit, advised Paul not to go up to Jerusalem (v. 4). And since Paul went there anyway, he would have acted contrary to the will of God. But what does Scripture actually say?

What is the import of the word "not" in verse 4? Is it an absolute interdiction? The answer is quite simple. The Greek has several words for "not," the chief ones being "ou" and "me." Now, "ou" expresses an absolute negation (as for instance in Matt. 4:4; 5:21), and "me" expresses a relative negation. Any believer can verify this by looking up the texts where "me" is used. Thus Matt. 10:5, "Go not into the way of the Gentiles" (were they never to go to them?); John 20:17, "Touch Me not" (when in verse 27 He asks Thomas to touch Him); Acts 1:4, "(He) commanded them that they should not depart from Jerusalem" (were they to remain there forever?).

We see therefore that "me" is relative, temporary. Well, this is the word that is used in Acts 21:4. Is it not clear, then, that the Spirit was saying in that passage to tarry 7 days in Tyre before boarding a ship departing for Jerusalem? Then, after they had completed these 7 days, they departed, v. 5, a decision in complete agreement with the will of God. It was men who wanted to detain Paul and prevent him from accomplishing His will; but he did not allow himself to be persuaded, and finally they said: "The will of the Lord be done," v. 14.

This is another example of the precision of the Word. If we hold fast the form of sound words, 2 Tim. 1:13, we will be less inclined to accuse the Apostles when one of their actions does not agree with our theory.

MORE ON THE PLAN OF GOD

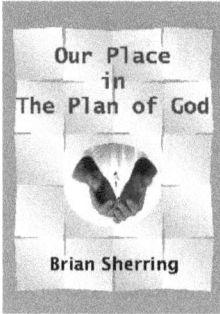

Our Place in The Plan of God
By Brian Sherring

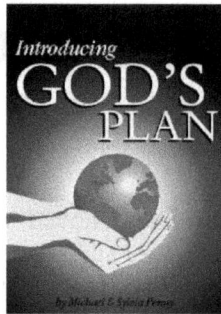

Introducing God's Plan
By Michael & Sylvia Penny

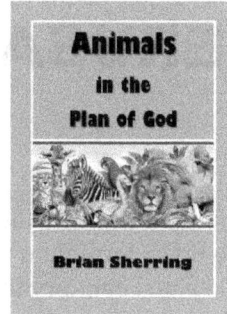

Animals in the Plan of God
By Brian Sherring

God's Amazing Plan
By David Groves

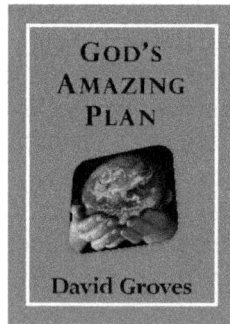

Further details of the above book can be seen on **www.obt.org.uk**

They can be ordered from that website and from

The Open Bible Trust
Fordland Mount, Upper Basildon,
Reading, RG8 8LU, UK.

They are also available as eBooks from Amazon and Apple,
and as paperbacks from Amazon.

FREE MAGAZINE

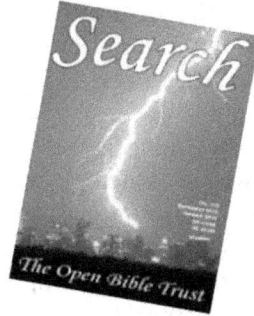

ABOUT THE AUTHOR

"From the stagnant pools of tradition to the fountainhead of truth" might be an apt description of the path outlined by the author in his exploration of the Scriptures.

Bishop Butler has stated that the only way to study the Word of God is the way in which physical science is studied. In his *Analogy*, Part II, ch. 3, he says: "As it is owned, the whole scheme of Scriptures is not yet understood, so if it ever comes to be understood before the restitution of all things, and without miraculous interpositions, *it must be in the same way* as natural knowledge is come at, by the continuance and progress of learning and liberty, and by particular persons attending to, comparing, and pursuing intimations scattered up and down it, and which are overlooked and disregarded by the generality of the world."

Undertaking a systematic study of the Bible as a scientist examines a new specimen, without preconceived ideas, the author approached his study with a provisional belief in the unity and veracity of the Bible as a working hypothesis, allowing Scripture to explain itself. The author takes the reader with him along the path which he himself followed.

Born in Antwerp, Belgium in 1888, the author, S. Van Mierlo, trained in the scientific disciplines, eventually becoming responsible for the direction of research activities in the laboratories of an international telecommunications corporation in five European countries. To these responsibilities he added extensive research in archeology, theology, philosophy, ancient writings, and records of abnormal phenomena. A frequent visitor to the British Museum Library and other centers of information, the author met and consulted with many biblical authorities in several countries. He spoke several languages and knew Greek and Hebrew.

As a result of his studies he was led to publishing a number of books and pamphlets, mostly in the French language. He lectured for private and religious groups in Europe, and was for a time coeditor of a monthly devoted to Bible exposition in the Dutch language.

This book is a translation of one of the author's works for English-speaking readers.

****

[1] This method is more fully expounded in <u>Science, Reason, and Faith.</u> With basic elements as a starting point, one strives to make a synthesis, to reconstruct the "whole." If one comes across difficulties, apparent contradictions or even seeming impossibilities, one does not abandon the preliminary faith and branch off in one or another direction from the path of truth. Far from it! Instead, one recognizes that these obstacles must be due to one's own imperfection – one's tentative hypothesis has deviated from the truth. The "child" and the man of science then abandon such false concepts, they "repent," confess their weakness, and reach a better solution.

[2] This expression shows that the word "eternal" as a translation of "aionion" does not have the meaning we usually attach to it. Taking "eternal" in the habitual sense, the expression "times eternal" would be a contradiction. (See Appendix 1: <u>Eternity.</u> See also 1 Cor. 2:7 "pro ton aionion," i.e.: "before (the) times of the ages," as in 2 Tim. 1:9.

[3] Col. 1:15. See also Heb. 1:3, "express image," and John 17:5.

[4] Compare, for instance, Isa. 6:1-10 with John 12:41; Isa. 43:15, 44:6 with John 1:50, 12:13, etc., Isa. 43:11 with Acts 4:12 etc.; Isa. 45:22 with John 12:47; Isa. 45:23 with Phil. 2:10, 11; Ex. 34:6, 7 with Mark 2:5. See also John 20:28; 21:7; Rev. 1:8; Isa. 41:4, 44:6, 48:12.

[5] Gen. 16:7; 18:10-24 (see John 8:56); 22:11; Ex. 3:2-14. The Lord Frequently says: "ego eimi," **"I am,"** as in John 8:58.

[6] See Rom. 9:5; John 1:1; 5:18; 8:58; 10:30; 17:5; Titus 2:13, 3:4; Phil. 2:6; Col. 2:9; Heb. 1:8-10; 1 John 5:20.

[7] Scripture always uses the expression "first born" to indicate a superior position. In Col. 1:15 it is the pre-eminence of the Son over the whole creation; in Col. 1:18 and Rev. 3:14, over death (for He is the resurrection and the life, John 11:25).

[8] Col. 1:17. In Col. 1:18 the Greek "arche," translated "beginning," also has the sense of "authority" or power," as in Col. 1:16.

[9] The creature has no life in itself: it is mortal, subject to death. God can bring it to immortality – this was necessary even without the fall and sin. The dead do not live, but continue to exist in another state. They may live again through resurrection; Scripture does not speak of a "natural" immortality.

[10] The Greek text of 1 Cor. 8:6 uses the preposition "ek," and one can translate thus: "...there is but one God, the Father, out of Whom are all things."

[11] Questions relating to freedom, predestination, and election are discussed in our work <u>The Way of Salvation.</u>

[12] For the problem of evil, see <u>Science, Reason, and Faith.</u>

[13] A great deal of this literature is examined by **Zockler** in <u>Gesch. Der Beziehungen zw. Theol. U. Naturwiss.</u>

[14] "Katabole" is used 10 times, translated by "foundation." The texts may be grouped in two series according to whether the reference is made to <u>before</u> or <u>since</u> the katabole:

> **Before:** John 17:24; Eph. 1:4; 1 Pet. 1:20.
> **Since:** Matt. 13:35; 25:34; Luke 11:50; Heb. 4:3; 9:26;

Rev. 13:8; 17:8. Without any doubt, the verb kataballo means "to cast down," as in 2 Cor. 4:9 and Rev. 12:10. In human literature and the dictionaries, the word katabole is used for "foundation," but it would be more logical to retain, in the Scriptures, the meaning of "destruction." which is closer to the etymological meaning of the word. Besides, for "foundation" the Greek verb "themelioo" is available.

[15] Gen. 6:2; Job. 1:6; 2:1; 38:7; Ps. 29:1; 89:7.

[16] Job 5:1; 15:15; Ps. 89:6, 8; Dan. 4:13; 8:13; Jude 14.

[17] Gen. 3:24; Eze. 9 & 10. They are also called "living creatures," Rev. 4:6.

[18] Dan. 12:1; 10:21; 1 Thess. 4:16; Jude 9: Rev. 12:7. Note that there is only one Archangel, and that he is "the great prince which standeth for the children of Israel."

[19] He was a model of "perfection" in his sphere, but not absolutely perfect.

[20] Note that the "garden of God" (Eze. 12:14) is not identical to "a garden eastward in Eden," Gen. 2:8, which does not belong to primitive creation.

[21] Eze. 28:12-17. See Dan. 10:13; Eph. 2:2 for two other cases where the word "prince" indicates spiritual beings. See Ex. 24:10, 17 for a vision of glittering stones near the throne of God.

[22] 1 John 3:8. This "beginning" is not that of creation, but of his fall, Eze. 28:15.

[23] It is quite possible that there were also some who wanted to remain in their imperfect original state, and others who without opposing God wanted to progress, but without Him. During the ages which follow the age of primitive creation, we will see examples of these two attitudes among men: the indifference and those who want to be justified by their works.

[24] We state this based on the Greek text of Heb. 11:3 which says, literally: "the eons were prepared anew" rather than "the worlds were framed." In fact, the verb "katartizo" has the more particular sense of "to prepare anew," as we may see for instance in Mat

. 4:21 (mending), 21:16 (prepare); Heb. 10:5 (prepared). There is no question of a simple "repair."

[25] The Hebrew word "yom," translated "day," does not necessarily indicate a period of 12 or 24 hours; it is often used for a period of an undetermined duration. The Hebrew word "boker," translated "morning," has the general meaning of "beginning." See for instance Ps. 90:14 (early, in the morning). The word translated by "evening" indicates an ending Eccl. 11:6, which is speaking about the beginning and ending of life. Note that in the first chapter of Genesis there is no question of nights: it is referring to long periods of Divine activity, thus of "light," in contrast with the "darkness," Gen. 1:2, which resulted from satanic action. More details are given in The Divine Revelation

[26] In the case where each of the six "days" would have been a period of 24 hours, the chaos would still have subsisted some 4000 to 5000 years before Jesus Christ; but the firm data from science show that the chaos dates from several hundred millions of years ago. On the other hand, if one believes in the inspiration of the Scriptures, Adam was created 4,000 to 5,000 years before Jesus Christ for in his genealogy it is impossible to insert anyone else (as it is possible in the case of other Biblical genealogies). For details, please refer to The Divine Revelation.

[27] 2 Cor. 4:4; Col. 1:15; Heb. 1:3.

[28] The phrase "thou shalt surely die" in Gen. 2:17 translates more literally as "dying thou shalt die," which indicates a process requiring a certain amount of time.

[29] See Mal. 3:6; Num. 23:19; James 1:16, 17. This does not mean that God does not deal with His creatures in different ways. He does not change in His Being.

[30] Let us remember not to confuse life with existence; the dead man still **exists**.

[31] See Heb. 4:4. "Katapauo" means "to cease" and not "to rest." The same applies to the Hebrew word. God does not rest; on the contrary, He "works until now" (John 5:17).

[32] See Matt. 25:34.

[33] In Rev. 4:6-9, the word "beasts" means "living creatures;" in Gen. 14:7 the Hebrew expression "the whole field" means "all the country," as it does in Num. 21:20, Judges 20:6; Ruth 1:1, 2, 6, 22, 2:6; 1 Sam. 27:5, 7, 11, etc.

[34] 2 Cor. 11:3; Rev. 20. Just as Nero is called "lion," 2 Tim. 4:17, and Herod is called "fox," Luke 13:32.

[35] Gen. 3 verses 14 and 15 use figures of speech, as does Ps. 44:25. The expression "upon thy belly shalt thou go" expresses a disillusion and an abasement. See Prov. 20:17 and Ps. 72:9 for similar expressions.

[36] Or body is largely composed of colloids, and their flocculation seems to be the basic cause of disease and death. Good hygiene may retard this flocculation but we cannot avoid it.

[37] Rom. 3:23. Note that "come short of" or "fail" (hustereo) does not imply a complete lack. See Heb. 12:15.

[38] See The Way of Salvation.

[39] The expression "son of Elohim," thus of God as Creator, is never used in the OT to designate men, but always to indicate angels. See Job 1:6; 2:1; 38:7; Ps. 29:1; 89:7; Dan. 3:25, 28. Nothing permits us to give another meaning. On the other hand, "sons of Jehovah," the God of covenants, is used in Deut. 14:1 to designate Jews. See also Isa. 43:3-6. In the NT Adam is called "son of God" because he was created directly by God. Those who have become "new creatures" are also called "sons of God." What Gen. 6 says of the angels is confirmed by Jude 6, 7. Note that for "habitation," the Greek uses "house" or "dwelling place" in 2 Cor. 5:2. They had left the heavenly sphere. The Greek text speaks of "going after different flesh" they had taken a carnal form and came to the daughters of men who had a flesh of different nature.

We also know that angels are called "spirits," Ps. 104:4; Heb. 1:7 14, and it is very likely that 1 Pet. 3:19, 20 and 2 Pet. 2:4, 5 give us further indications about those "sons of Elohim" and their progeny who were still living in Noah's day. These spirits were thrown "in prison," "cast down to hell and delivered into pits of darkness" until the day of judgment. The Lord, after His resurrection, went to them to proclaim His victory. Note that the word "spirit" never designates a man except after resurrection when the body is governed entirely by the spirit. The dead, besides, are not in prison but in Hades. In 1 Pet. 3:19 the word "preached" is not the translation of euangelizo, i.e., "to announce the good news," but of kerusso, i.e., "to proclaim, as a herald." This word indicates the behavior, not the contents of the message. From these "sons of Elohim" came the race of the Nephilim and those of the "giants," Gen.6:4. See also Appendix 3.

[40] Gen. 2:5, 6. The word "eretz," translated "earth" in verses 5 and 6 is translated "land" in verses 11, 12, and 13.

[41] Gen. 9:1-17. It should be noted that Noah and his sons were not to "subdue" the earth, as Adam should have done, Gen. 1:28. This was not ordained by God for the humanity of the present age. Any would-be world conqueror would thus be acting against the will of God. This mission is reserved for Christ in the coming age.

[42] For details see "The Divine Revelation."

[43] See Chapter XVII and Appendix 9 of "The Divine Revelation."

[44] The "promised land" extends from the "river of Egypt" to the Euphrates, Gen. 15:18. The "river" (nahar) is the Nile, not to be confused with the wadi el-Arich, the "stream" (nahar) of Egypt of 1 Kings 8:65 which is situated south-west of Gaza, Joshua 15:47. This land has never been possessed by Israel to this day.

[45] The expression "for ever" in Gen. 13:15 should be read: "during the olam," and instead of "everlasting" in Gen. 17:8 the Hebrew text says "relative to the olam." It is about the olam, or the age to come, when the promises will be realized. The cont'd. Greek word corresponding to "olam" is "aion." See Matt. 12:32 and Luke 20:34, 35 for the distinction between the present age and that to come. See also Appendix 1.

[46] Gal. 3:6 shows us that Christ is The Posterity, pre-eminently. All blessings (earthly for **the nation** and heavenly to all who are justified by faith) can only come through a spiritual communion with Christ. The heavenly posterity made up of the sons (huios) of God, baptized in Christ, crucified and having died with Him, Rom. 6:3-8; Gal. 3:26-29, finds itself in such a communion with God, in Him – i.e.: in relation to this spiritual position – there is neither Jew nor Greek neither bond nor free, neither male nor female. But as far as earthly life is concerned, these divisions remain.

Rom. 9:6-8 shows that the children (tekna) of the flesh are not necessarily children (tekna) of God and of the promise and do not constitute the true posterity of Abraham. (They are called "sons of the race of Abraham" in Acts 13:26.) The earthly posterity forming **a nation** will be the true posterity, the true Israel, only through its faith in the Messiah, that is, the Christ. See also Rom. 2:28, 29; 9:7, and Heb. 11:18. That is the Israel of God, Gal. 6:16, in contrast to Israel after the flesh, 1 Cor. 10:18.

[47] Note that the word translated "depart" can be understood in the sense of "spread." This verse thus says that the kingdom will not spread farther than the land of Judah until Shiloh, the true King, will have returned.

[48] See note 39 Chapter III, and Appendix 3.

[49] It has been said that the word "neighbor" in Lev. 19:18 designates only the sons of Israel. However, verse 34 adds: "The stranger that dwelleth with you shall be unto you as one born among you, and thou shalt love him as thyself."

[50] Matt. 22:36-40. The Law also required sanctification, Lev. 11:44, 45; 19:2; 1 Pet. 1:16, and circumcision of the heart, Jer. 9:25, 26.

[51] See for instance 1 Chron. 29:17-19; 2 Chron. 16:9; Jer. 7:22, 23; Hos. 6:6; Amos 5:21-24; Micah 6:6-8; Zech. 8:17; Isa 58:4-10. They expressed themselves so strongly that some have concluded that the

ceremonies had never been instituted by God. Thus Barnabas, who wrote near the end of the first century, thought that all this must be spiritualized, that the Jews had misunderstood the Law. (Epistle of Barnabas, pages 6, 9, 10, 11 and 15.) The ceremonies had no value of themselves, but they were needed as symbols of spiritual realities.

[52] The Hebrew words kopher and karphar are translated into many different words; the general meaning is: something which covers and protects. The Greek words hilasmost, hilaskomai, hisasterion that we meet in Luke 18:13; Rom. 3:25; Heb. 2:17; 9:5; 1 John 2:2; 4:10; agree with this meeting. All this merely "covers" the sin, Ps. 32:1, Rom. 4:7, or the sinner, but was not effective in itself. It was temporary, conditional, as was the "remission" or the "forgiveness" of sins. (See Proposition 14, "The Remission of sins…" under subtitle **"d. The Gospels"**.) The justice of God required punishment, but in the "time of His patience" He could temporarily postpone the punishment while waiting for the true Atoning Victim Who would blot out sin. We will see the development of this later.

[53] Rom. 6:14. It is important to see the difference between being "in" the law and "under" the law. Note that the Greek text of Rom. 2:12 and 3:19 does not say "under" the law but "in" the law. Since Israel had the knowledge of the will of God, through the law, they were "in" the Law, in their sphere. But in attempting to accomplish this Law by their own efforts, they placed themselves "under" the Law, as slaves.

[54] Gen. 17:7, 13, 19; 21:33; Ex. 27:21; 28:43; 29:28; 31:16, 17; Lev. 3:17; 23:14; etc.

[55] The matter of the observation of the Law in the future, by Jews who believe in Christ, will be examined later on. See also the answers to some objections in Appendix 5. We remind the reader that the method of scientific examination requires that certain data not be rejected because of traditional conceptions resulting from a theological system which perhaps should itself be revised. It is to be seen whether we can maintain the OT statements when we will examine the Gospels and the Epistles of the Apostle Paul.

[56] To the Jew, the OT is divided into 3 parts: the Law, the Prophets, and the Psalms, as so named in Luke 24:44. Here follows a list of the books contained in each part:
1. The Law: Genesis, Exodus, Leviticus, Numbers, Deuteronomy.
2. The Prophets: Joshua, Judges, Samuel, Kings, Isaiah, Jeremiah, Ezekiel, and the twelve "minor" prophets.
3. The Psalm: Psalms, Proverbs, Job, Song of Solomon, Ruth, Lamentations, Ecclesiastes, Esther, Daniel, Ezra-Nehemiah, Chronicles.

[57] Some find it impossible to admit that God could have ordered the extermination of entire peoples. But when one comes to realize the nature of this population and the danger faced by Israel, one can understand. But in such a case, only God could judge. See Appendix 3.

[58] For example: an evil spirit, 1 Sam. 16:14; 18:10; 19:9; Goliath, 1 Sam. 17:4; the giant Ishbi-benob, 2 Sam. 21:16; Saph, and the man with six fingers and six toes, 2 Sam. 21:20.

[59] See, for example, the marriage of Jehoram and Athaliah and the massacre of all his brothers, 2 Chron. 21:4; the slaying of all the eldest sons of Jehoram, 2 Chron. 22:1; the destruction of all the royal seed by Athaliah, 2 Chron. 22:10, excepting Joash who remained hidden for six years in the house of God, 2 Chron. 22:12. We clearly see that if the posterity of the woman was not annihilated, this was due to a continual succession of Divine interventions.

[60] It has often been said that this is when "the time of the nations," mentioned in Luke 21:24 begins, and is lasting until now, until that future time when the nation would again become "Ammi." But it must not be forgotten, as we will observe in note 74, Chapter IV, Section g, that the Prophets are completely silent about anything that relates to the times when Israel has no national and religious existence. It follows that any mention of "the times of the nations" must refer to a time frame during which the nations oppress and persecute Israel **as a nation of God**, while in their land. This, for instance, was the case in the circumstances during which Eze. 30:3 was speaking, but not in the present case, where Israel is restored nationally but not yet on a religious basis as long as the Temple is not rebuilt.

As to "the times of the nations" of Luke 21:24, this concerns the 42 months (corresponding to the last half of the seventieth week of years and to the three-and-a-half times of Dan. 7:25; 9:27; 12:7; and Rev. 12:14 and 13:5) preceding the end of the present age and ending with the day of the Lord. In fact, in Rev. 11:2 we read that the nations "shall tread under foot the holy city forty and two months," which corresponds to Luke 21:24: "…Jerusalem shall be trodden down of the Gentiles, until the "times of the Gentiles" shall be fulfilled."

[61] John 1:17. This does not mean that they had to wait for the coming of Christ in order to obtain this grace, several have received it before that time. The Work of Christ is, for us, accomplished in time. But God is not subject to time, and in its spiritual reality the Work of Christ is independent of time.

The notion of grace and the work of Christ, which enables the dispensation of grace, distinguishes the teachings of the Word of God from the "religious" or moral systems who sometimes prescribe that which is good to do, but do not provide the means to accomplish it. More often, they aim at the improvement of man through his own efforts, which must necessarily lead to antichristianism and failure.

[62] In our time also, it is important to reckon with all this. Many men are making "miracles," or pretending to make them. But those miracles do not necessarily come from God. The godless, "whose coming is after the working of Satan with all power and signs and lying wonders," 2 Thess. 2:9, will also claim to do miracles. Besides, man can, by using nothing more than his sensitive and higher faculties, accomplish much that may **appear** to be miraculous. It is the written Word, understood with the help and enlightenment from the Holy Spirit, which must remain the touchstone. One must always beware of any man or any organization who base their teachings on events said to be miraculous. To the contrary, we have, above all, all the true doctrine in the Scriptures, and this is the one which enables the man who loves the Truth to judge a "miraculous" event. Let us also recall 2 Cor. 11 and Gal. 1:8, 9.

[63] It has been suggested that the idea of an earthly kingdom could have provided Pilate with a good reason to condemn Jesus Christ. This would indeed have been the case if it had been about a <u>human</u> kingdom, like all the other ones. If Pilate had been convinced of this, he would not have hesitated to crucify the One who pretended to be King. But Pilate, perhaps under the influence of his wife, Matt. 27:19, and by the Jews' attitude, understood that it was not about a kingdom that would be set up by men. However, he was not convinced that Jesus was the Son of God, John 18:37. So he chose to remain neutral as far as possible.

[64] Matt. 24:4-21, 30. In his time, John the Baptist could already speak of the wrath to come," Matt. 3:6, 7, for the Kingdom was near, and the great tribulation also.

[65] In Mark 9:1, the "some of them" who would see the Kingdom of God coming with power before dying, were very likely Peter, James, and John, who had received a vision of the Lord as He would appear at the Kingdom. The generation of Matt. 24:34 and Mark 13:30 refers to Israel after its conversion, the **nation** which will "bring forth the fruits," Matt. 21:43. Matt. 24:33 clearly shows that this is about the generation who will see "all these things," that is to say, the events which announce the fairly near coming of the Son of man, Matt. 24:15 for instance.

[66] It is true that the last twelve verses of Mark 16 are not found in two of the major manuscripts (Vaticanus and Sinaiticus). However, the former shows a blank space at this location, and in the latter the last two pages are written in a larger writing. Thus both show something abnormal at

this place. Also, most of the other manuscripts, some 600 of them, and the most ancient versions (in Syriac) do include these 16 verses. And Jerome, who had access to manuscripts older than those we know, added them in his Latin version.

[67] See Matt. 9:36 and the Prophets: Jer. 23:3, 4; Eze. 34:12-16; 22-24. Also Matt. 15:24; John 10:11. Only faithful Jews are called sheep. Jesus Christ is the "good Shepherd," John 10:11, and Isa. 40:11; Ps. 23. He is called "the great Shepherd" in Heb. 13:20, and "the chief Shepherd" in 1 Pet. 5:4, two epistles addressed to Christian Jews.

[68] Deut. 6:5; Lev. 19:18. It may be interesting at this point to recall the parallel between the "sermon on the mount" and Ps. 15. Compare Matt. 5:3-12 with Ps. 15:1; Matt. 5:13-16:34 with Ps. 15:2; Matt. 7:1-5 and 5:43-48 with Ps. 15:3; Matt. 7:15-23 and 5:33-37 with Ps. 15:4; Matt. 5:33-42 and 7:24-27 with Ps. 15:5. We recall also Note 49 in Chapter IV, b.

[69] The Greek word translated "judging" has a wider meaning, and can be translated by "leading;" this was the duty of the OT "Judges."

[70] "Whatsoever" refers, not to men, but to actions. See Matt. 18:15-18. They were to guide men as to what they must observe, to lead them in God's ways. This is the opposite of what the Pharisees were doing, for these were "binding heavy burdens, grievous to be borne," Matt. 23:4.

[71] See Acts 2:38; 8:16; 10:48; 19:5; Rom. 6:3; 1 Cor. 1:17 where some other expression is always used. How can one possibly apply Matt. 28:19 indiscriminately when Paul says in 1 Cor. 1:17 that Christ did not send him to baptize?

[72] The word church or assembly comes from the Greek "ekklesia" which indicates a group of chosen men, and corresponds to the Hebrew "kahal." The people of Israel are called "kahal" (a multitude), having been chosen from among other peoples, Gen. 28:3. This word is frequently used in the OT. See, for example, Gen. 49:6; Deut. 18:16; 31:30; Josh. 8:35; Judg. 21:8; Ps. 22:23, 26. In the NT, "ekklesia" often designates local assemblies, Acts 5:11; 8:3; 1 Cor. 4:17; etc. It is also used of the goldsmiths' guild of Ephesus. The Apostle Paul uses it to indicate a special assembly, the Church of the Mystery, Eph. 1:22.

[73] See, for instance, Hosea 1:11: "Then shall the children of Judah and the children of Israel be gathered together," and Ps. 22:22, 25: "In the midst of the congregation (assembly) will I praise Thee," "My praise shall be of Thee in the great congregation."

[74] Rev. 1:18. For the expression "gates of Hell" see Isa. 38:10; Ps. 9:13; 107:18. This is about the power of Hades to keep the dead, or also of the lack of power of the dead to return to life. The verb translated "to prevail"

is also used in Luke 23:23 and indicates that the one is stronger than the other. The Lord holds the keys of hell and of death, Rev. 1:18, and when He will release the dead, as He has been released, the power of Hades will not have the upper hand.

[75] See, for instance, Isa. 49:18; 54:4-10; 62:4, 5; Jer. 2:2; 3:1-14; 31:32; Eze. 16:8-13; Hosea 2:18; etc. No difficulty arises because Israel was already called the "bride" or "wife" in the OT and the marriage of the Lamb with Israel is yet to come. Indeed, Deut. 22:23, 24 as well as Matt. 1:18, 20 show that a woman "betrothed" is already legally called "wife."

[76] It has been said that the precepts of the Gospels are very good, but not practicable. Now, it is true that certain precepts are not suitable to our period, and those which are applicable for all times, such as charity, can only be put into practice through a spiritual action within us. So we should not expect them to be observed by men in general.

[77] See Isa. 55:3; Jer. 31:31-34; Eze. 37:24-28.

[78] 1 Cor. 10:16. We know that the ritual of the Jewish Passover involved four cups, two of them before the meal (these were not actually part of the ritual), and the two others after the meal. The third cup was called "the cup of blessing." The (flat) loaves of bread were broken up in pieces which were eaten several times during the ritual. The Lord followed this custom and has neither innovated nor instituted anything; He accomplished and explained.

[79] Eze. 45:21. See also Ex. 12:14; 13:9.

[80] Matt. 26:29. Literally: "I drink it new," that is to say, in a new manner."

[81] Ex. 12:43-48. To take part in it, they had to be circumcised and so be incorporated into Israel. One could, of course, wonder if the Gentile believer in Christ must still be considered as a "foreigner" since Paul seems to speak of "the cup of blessing" to all men, and of breaking of bread in his first Epistle to the Corinthians. But is he really speaking to all Christians in Chapters 10 and 11? He begins these chapters by saying: "Brethren, I would not that ye should be ignorant how that all our fathers were under the cloud, and all passed through the sea; and were baptized unto Moses in the cloud and in the sea..." This is about Jewish brethren, "to whom pertaineth the adoption, and the glory, and the covenants, and the giving of the law, and the service of God, and the promises; whose are the fathers...", Rom. 9:4. When Paul was speaking about Jewish worship or service, it was obvious, to those of his time, that he was addressing Christian Jews only; and we could not wish for a clearer statement than that. Here also, it is only in the case where Israel would no longer have been the elected people, but would have been replaced by a "Church", that all this could have been "spiritualized" and applied to

that Church. The careful reader will have noticed that in 1 Cor. 11:25, 26 it is not said: "Do this until He comes," but as long as the Passover could be celebrated during the times preceding His coming, i.e. as long as Israel remained the elected people, they had to do this in remembrance of Him every time they would drink the cup in the prescribed manner.

[82] Matt. 18:27. The inspired text here uses the verb "aphiemi," translated by "loosen" and "forgive."

[83] For instance: Eph. 4:32. Here "forgiving" is the translation of the verb "charizomai" See also 1 Cor. 2:12, where "freely" means "given as an act of grace."

[84] For instance: 2 Sam. 12:13; 2 Chron. 7:13, 14; Ps. 32:5; Isa. 6:5-7; 43:25 26; Acts 10:43.

[85] Deut. 30:6; Ps. 51:7, 12; Isa. 44:3; 57:15; Jer. 24:7; 31:33; 32:39; Eze. 11:19; 18:31; 36:25-27; Joel 2:28-32.

[86] Matt. 19:28. The word "palingenesia" ("new birth") in the Greek text is translated "the regeneration."

[87] Their life does not cease after this age (see Luke 20:36), but it will then have other characteristics, those conforming to the following age. Thus, the qualification "eonian" does not limit but rather characterizes.

[88] The Greek text does not use the preposition "en" but "eis" (up to).

[89] 1 Thess. 4:17. This is about those who will have part in the heavenly eonian life. They are called "sons." See The Teachings of the Apostle Paul.

[90] One might point to Acts 1:5, where it is stated that they would be "baptized with the Holy Ghost" not many days hence, in order to insinuate that the Apostles could have been mistaken. But we have just read that Luke 24:45 said that their understanding was already opened **that they might understand the Scriptures**. The baptism "with the Holy Ghost" was, in Acts 1:8, related to the "power from on high," Luke 24:49, which enables them to be witnesses, to perform wonders and miracles which demonstrated – as it did during the time of the Acts – that the Kingdom was near. Besides, John 20:22 shows that they already "received the Holy Ghost."

[91] Acts 8:26, 29, 39; 10:3, 19, 22 (the angel is also called "Spirit"); 11:12, 13; 27:23.

[92] Acts 4:29-31; 14:3; Rom. 15:19; 1 Cor. 12:28; 2 Cor. 12:12; Heb. 2:3, 4; 6:5

[93] It is true that **during** Acts Paul suffered "a thorn in the flesh," 2 Cor. 12:7; Gal. 4:14. But this was precisely something quite exceptional in that time. And so, since the Lord did not remove it, in spite of his triple prayers, he received a message from the Lord to make him understand

that this was necessary in order that he be not "exalted above measure" because of the excellence of his revelations. The rule was: healing. What is striking is that after Acts not a single case of healing is mentioned, nor are there any of the peculiarities which characterized the period of Acts.
[94] Let us note that all had heard the words of the Lord through Paul when he was performing special miracles, Acts 19:10-12.
[95] Up to the beginning of the time of Acts, men could be divided into Jew and heathen. With the advent of the first Christians among the nations, there began to be formed what has been called "tertius genus," i.e., a third "race." That was one of the events which necessitated the meeting mentioned in Acts 15. Peter had learned, since his contact with Cornelius, that these Christians should no longer be reckoned as being "impure." They were, in fact, no longer pagans worshipping idols, God having purified their hearts by faith, Acts 11:9 and 15:9. Consequently, while rigorously observing the Law, the Christian Jew could associate with the non-Jewish Christian. However, as with all proselytes, these Christians had to observe certain rules so as not to offend the Jews. Not all these rules are evidently applicable today.
[96] In Appendix 5 we examine the principal objections to this thesis which may appear to be a somewhat radical one. Here we will merely state that Rom. 10:4 is not in glaring contradiction with our conclusions. The Biblical sense of "For Christ" is the end of the law" is determined by the exact meaning of the word "end." Now, the inspired text uses the word "telos" which indicates a goal rather than the end of something, as clearly shown by texts such as Matt. 26:58 and Rom. 6:21. To indicate something which no longer exists, the word "peras" could have been used, as in Heb. 6:16 "an end (peras) of all strife."
[97] See 1 Cor. 11:25 and Heb. 10:3. The latter text gives an opportunity to reply to another objection. Verses 4 to 10 are cited to "prove" that all offerings are abolished, Christ having offered Himself once for all. However, this argument would prove too much. As a matter of fact, these verses are cited from Ps. 40:6. If one wishes to conclude therefrom that offerings are abolished, they should also not have existed when these words were written, that is, a long time before the cross. What is abolished is the Old Covenant; what is established, is the New Covenant. The Law is not abolished but accomplished by grace. They are no longer "under" the Law, but are still "in" the Law.
[98] Also Deut. 30:6; Ps. 51:7, 12; Isa. 57:15; Jer. 24:7; 31:33; 32:39; Eze. 11:19; 18:31.
[99] Acts 2:5, "Jews;" 2:14, "men of Judea;" 2:22, "men of Israel;" 2:36, "all the house of Israel." Note that the words "Parthians" and "Medes" in

v. 9, designate Jews or proselytes living in those parts. The "Grecians" in Acts 6:1 are Jews who have adopted some of the Greek customs and speak Greek. The expression "brethren" in Acts 6:3 was in current use among the Jews, see, for instance, Acts 2:29-36; 7:26, 37.

[100] Acts 2:47 reads: "And the Lord added to the church daily such as should be saved." But the word "church" does not appear in the principal manuscripts. Besides, as previously noted, the word "ekklesia" (or "kahal") was used to designate Jewish assemblies.

[101] Acts 9:15; 13:2; 22:21; Gal. 2:7-9; Eph. 3:8; 1 Tim. 2:7; 2 Tim. 1:11.

[102] Someone who occupies a higher position in the way of salvation is not exempt from concern for those who are at the beginning – on the contrary. See also Col. 1:28.

[103] The Apostles did not choose Matthias: they appointed, Acts 1:23, the only two who satisfied the conditions of verses 21 and 22. As to the drawing of lots, v. 26, that is how God wanted them to act in that type of situation: see Lev. 16:8-10; Num. 26:55; Neh. 10:34; Jonah 1:7; etc. This also shows that we must be very careful in making accusations, and that the circumstances of that period were very different from ours. The drawing of lots has never been ordained to us.

[104] Eph. 4:10, 11. The prophets, i.e. those who speak for God, mentioned here are not those of the OT. They are named after the Apostles.

[105] The part which concerns man personally in relation to God is for all, but the part which addresses man as a child of the elected people is not applicable to all.

[106] As an example, let's look at the Law given to Israel. It was the expression of God's will for that people and in those circumstances. But many commandments which are part of that Law also concern other men, and the whole constitutes a body of teachings necessary for all. On the other hand, certain indications – and in particular, the ceremonies – are not applicable to anyone. All, therefore, is good for us, but all does not necessarily apply to us. The same applies to other parts of the Word of God, and it is thus essential to correctly divide it, 2 Tim. 2:15, and to "approve the things that are more excellent," Rom. 2:18, or, in the spirit of the original text, "to distinguish things that differ."

[107] The fact that all that Paul was teaching could, at that time, be verified by the OT is demonstrated by the fact that, 25 years after Pentecost, the Jews from Berea searched the Scriptures, i.e. the OT, to see that "those things were so," Acts 17:10, 11. Up to the end of Acts, Paul witnessed to all, "saying none other things than those which the prophets and Moses did say should come…", Acts 26:22, 23.

[108] We intentionally do not use here the verb "to reveal" which should be reserved for that which God does, as the inspired text exemplifies.

[109] Before telling men how they should act, Scripture always presents a doctrine, i.e. what God has done for them, their privileges, and their responsibilities. See, for instance, Rom. 8:12; Eph. 4:1; Col. 3:1; Heb. 10:19.

[110] In his first epistle to the dispersion, Peter – alluding to Ex. 19:6; Isa. 61:6; 66:21 – calls the converted people of Israel, an **holy** nation, 1 Peter 2:9. The word "nation," "ethnos," can in no way be applied to a "church" made up of men from different nations. Similarly, in Matt. 21:43 the word "nation" necessarily designates Israel after their repentance.

[111] Eph. 1:3. The Greek text says: "Who hath blessed us with all spiritual blessings in the above-heavenly (spheres)." The expression "en tois epouraniois" (in the above-heavens) is used only by Paul (Eph. 1:3, 30; 2:6; 3:10; 6:12) and never during the time of Acts. The "above-heavenly" spheres were known (see, for instance, John 3:12: "of heavenly things," (Greek text: "epourania"), but this "residence" of God was at that time inaccessible. Further details are given in The Teachings of the Apostle Paul.

[112] We have seen how, during Acts, the visible Kingdom Church, made up of Christian Jews, began to be formed. This community of "Nazarenes," of which first-century writings tell us that James, the Lord's brother, was "bishop" at Jerusalem and of which Paul was considered – erroneously – to be the ringleader by Tertullus, Acts 24:5, was at the time a Jewish sect, Acts 24:14; 28:22, having its own (Christian) synagogues. This community thus formed a group separate from non-Jewish Christians.

In the time preceding the Kingdom, a similar group will be formed, and it is noteworthy that, in Israel's present state, there now already exists a "Judeo-Christian Community" which considers itself to be the first nucleus of the converted people of Israel, and which has its own synagogue, practices the Law as far as possible, and believes to have the mission of announcing the Gospel of the Kingdom.

[113] See for instance: Ps. 118:22; Isa. 9:5, 6; 53:10; 61:2; Dan. 9:26, 27; Hosea 2:13, 14; 3:4, 5; Amos 9:10, 11; Micah 5:2, 3; Hab. 2:13, 14; Zeph. 3:7, 8; Zech. 9:9, 10. There is no room in these texts for the present times while Israel is not the people of God.

[114] Matt 24:5, 11, 24, and see also 2 Pet. 2:1; 1 John 4:2, 3; 2 John; Jude, for the false prophets and teachers.

[115] The Hebrew word "satan" means "adversary." Satanic action must not be searched for specially in the crimes and evil morality, nor even in

atheism, but rather in that which concerns religion. Under cover of peace, progress, of a universal religion – thus under the appearances of an angel of light – he will seduce the entire world. His chief aim is always to oppose himself to Christ and the realization of the Divine plan, and thus also to the re-establishment of Israel and the coming of the Kingdom on earth.

[116] Rev. 1:10 does not say, in the Greek text, that John was taken up "in the Spirit" on the "Lord's day" (often taken to mean a Sunday), but that he was transported in the Spirit **in** that day of the Lord which the Prophets had said so much. He had a vision – mostly in symbolic form – of the events of the last years of the present age. The entire Revelation relates to yet future times, even to us. It is sometimes believed that verse 19 makes a distinction between the past, present, and future. But the Greek text does not say "and the things which are" but "what (they) are," that is to say, what they signify. The word "eisi," translated by "are," is used twice in the next verse, and one will readily see that the intended meaning is "signify" or "represent."

Comparisons between Rev. 2:13 and 13:2; 16:10, between 2:16 and 19:21, between 2:27 and 19:15, between 2:20-23 and 17:2, 4; 18:3, between 3:3 and 16:15, etc. also show that those first chapters concern the future and not the history of the "Church." Note the mention of "synagogue" and "Jews" in Rev. 2:9 and 3:9.

In 1:10, the Greek text does not use the usual expression "day of the Lord," but reads, rather: "a Lordly day," to place the emphasis on "day." Scripture has no special expression for "Sunday." See also Appendix 4.

[117] What is said in Revelation about Babylon cannot be applied to a purely symbolic "Babylon." Isa. 13:20 says that the Arabian shall not pitch tent there. Now, at the present time, a few Arabs are still living in the ruins. The great works being undertaken in Iraq, which include new highways, dams and other irrigation works, etc., will transform the country and could lead in a not too distant future to a reconstruction of a great center near the ruins of ancient Babylon.

[118] For example: Isa. 2:12, 17; 13:6-9; Joel 1:15; 2:1-28; 3:14; Zeph. 1:7, 14; Zech. 14:1. Sometimes, the reference is to a day already past, as in Jer. 46:10 and Eze. 30:3, where the Lord shows His power.

[119] Isa. 13:10; Joel 3:15; Zeph. 1:15; Zach. 14:6; Matt. 24:29; Acts 2:20; Rev. 6:12-14.

[120] Isa. 25:8; 26:19, 21; Dan. 12:2, 13; Eze. 32:12-14; 1 John 3:2, Rev. 14:13; 20:4.

[121] 1 Thess. 4:14; 1 Cor. 15:42-50; Rev. 11:12.

[122] We cannot here study in detail the question of resurrections. There is an interval between the translation of the "sons of God" and the Lord's descent, but that interval cannot be one of several years, as some believe. To go and meet someone means that one goes to meet him and return with him right away. Some believe that, based on 1 Thess. 1:10, the translation will precede the great tribulation. But the Greek text uses the word "ek," and should thus be read as: "Which delivered us **out of** the wrath to come." This word "ek" is used twice more in this same verse: "to wait for His Son "out of" the heaven" and "Whom He raised "out of" the dead." The Lord is in the heavens and has been among the dead. Similarly, those in question will be in the wrath, but will come out of it. Any other arguments are worthless.

Let us add that Paul, who was sure of taking part in the resurrection out of the dead, says, in Phil. 3:11, that he hopes to take part in what the Greek text calls "the out-resurrection out of the dead." This is therefore another resurrection, doubtless an individual one, of those who have reached the final goal of the way of salvation and find themselves in the position of "perfect man," Eph. 4:13: they will appear with Him in glory, Col. 3:4.

[123] "The renewing of all things" is the translation of the Greek word "palingenesia," translated by "regeneration" in Titus 3:5. This corresponds to "gennao anothen" (new birth) in John 3:3-7: it is a new birth from above.

[124] Acts 3:21. Before the "Comforter" could come, and before the national new birth of Israel could come, the death of the Lord had first to take place, John 16:7. This new birth was to come only through His resurrection, 1 Pet. 1:3, 23. Pentecost would have been followed by the Kingdom on earth – it only lacked the repentance of Israel (acts 3:19-21).

[125] For instance: Ps. 2:28, 29; 24:1, 8, 10; 33:10, 11; 45:2, 3, 7; 72:8, 11; 93:1, 2; 97:1, 6, 9; Gen. 49:10. See also the Prophets.

[126] Ps. 47:2-9; 48:1, 10; 50:2; 66:4, 7; 100:1-5; 113:4; 150:6.

[127] 2 Sam. 7:16; Jer. 30:9, Eze. 34:23; 37:24.

[128] Isa. 60:22; Jer. 31:27, 28; Eze. 36:9-11; Mic. 4:6, 7; Zech. 8:4-6; Deut. 7:12-15.

[129] Deut. 30:6; Ps. 51:12; Isa. 44:3; Jer. 24:7; 31:33; 32:39; Eze. 11:19; 18:31; 36:25-27; Joel 2:28-32.

[130] Isa. 33:24; 43:24, 25; Jer. 31:34; Eze.16:60-63; 36:29; Zech. 13:1.

[131] Isa. 2:2; Jer. 30:18, 19; Eze. 40 to 46; Zech. 14:21; Mal. 3:3, 4.

[132] Ex. 19:6; Isa. 61:6; 66:21; 1 Pet. 2:9; Rev. 1:6.

[133] Ps 96:3; 98:2; Isa. 2:2, 3; 52:10; Jer. 3:17; Zech. 2:11; 8:13-23; 14:16, 17.

[134] Ps. 96:3; 98:2; Isa. 2:2, 3; 52:10; Jer. 3:17; Zech. 2:11; 8:13-23; 14:16, 17.

[135] Rev. 20:10. The Greek text says that he will be tormented there during the eons of eons i.e. during the 4th and 5th eons. See also Eze. 28:18, 19 and Appendix 1.

[136] The "above-heavenly" sphere, however, becomes accessible only after the time of Acts.

[137] Rev. 21:1. We have already noted, in Chapter IVc, that the new heavens and the new earth of Isa. 65:17 are not the same as those of Rev. 21. The heavens and earth of the 4th age are "new" compared to those of the 3rd age (our present age), and those of the 5th age are new compared to those of the 4th; but the change from the 4th to the 5th is far more radical. The Companion Bible brings out the following contrasts between the two Jerusalems in those two texts:

	Isa. 65	Rev. 21
Name	Jerusalem	New Jerusalem
Position	on a mountain	coming from heaven
Privileges	v. 18-20	v. 4
Characteristics	sinners, Temple	no sinners, no Temple
State	buildings, plantations	perfect

[138] In Rev. 21, it must be carefully observed that from verses 6 to 8, and at verses 24 and 27, John interrupts his description of the conditions during the 5th age; he then speaks of the nations and the kings of the 4th age, saying that nothing that was defiled in the 4th age will survive and enter into the City of the 5th age. The Greek word translated "anathema" is actually "katathema," which is much more radical than anathema.

[139] The Greek verb for "healing" is "therapeuo" which has a wide range of meanings. This can readily be seen from Acts 17:25 where "therapeuo" is variously translated "worshipped" or "served." In Rev. 22:2 it is not the verb but the noun "therapeia" that is used. This word is found only in the following verses: Matt. 24:25 (household); Luke 9:11 (healed); Luke 12:42 (household); and Rev. 22:2. The general meaning is "help" or assistance."

[140] The Greek text of Heb. 1:8 says: "Thy throne, O God, is unto the age of the age." This refers to the throne of the Son, which will remain until the end of the last age, the 5th age.

[141] See The Teachings of the Apostle Paul and The Way of Salvation.

[142] Col. 1:20. This text is taken as a basis by some Christians to claim that all creatures will be reconciled one day. However, this text simply says

that it pleases God to fully reconcile all with Him through Christ. Scripture selects its expressions very carefully when speaking about the destiny of men. It gives the outline of the purposes of God, and goes into greater detail when it is dealing with matters of major importance to us. While it is true that it does not mention unending tortures, it is equally true that it never states that all will one day be reconciled. One can understand the Word's prudence, and it would be desirable that men remain silent whenever God has not spoken.

To terrify men with an endless hell is no more dangerous than to promise to all that Judas, and even Satan himself will one day be reconciled with God. There is also a middle road: annihilation of non-believers. We prefer not to try to find a solution when God appears to remain silent; nor do we accept an alternative such as: "It must be either this or that." God has a thousand solutions where we do not see any. Ignorance is sometimes necessary; we have seen this during Acts: the Apostles were to proclaim the Kingdom as being near while God knew that Israel would be set aside. Without ignorance, they could not have delivered their message effectively, knowledge in this case would have been harmful to all. When God is silent, so should we be.

To those who, in spite of everything, must have an answer, we suggest a thorough study of the Word, trying to understand and live all the rest of the purposes of God – after this, they may possibly find the solution.

[143] Note that the Word never speaks of the resurrection of the flesh, i.e. of that which is solely material, but rather of man as a whole.

[144] It is known that Spiritism, Theosophy, and other anti-Christian groups deny the resurrection of the body and pretend that the dead are "spirits" without bodies. This is one more reason to beware of tradition. If one believes that the dead are truly dead and not living, and that they are in Hades with their bodies until resurrection, one is shielded against demoniac seductions in these matters because it is the Word which protects us.

[145] The following is a partial reproduction of Appendices 6 and 7 of the The Divine Revelation.

[146] See for instance the book Rephaim by Dr. P. Karge, 1917, and Geographie de la Palestine by Abel, 1933.

[147] The book of Jubilees (29:9 10), speaking of the departure of Abraham from Mesopotamia and of his covenant with Laban, mentions the Rephaim and says that they are giants of up to 3 meters tall.

[148] The Bible sometimes speaks of the "sons of Jehovah" (and not Elohim) to indicate Israelites: Deut. 14:1; Isa. 43:3, 6.

[149] See Job 1:6; 2:1; 38:7; Ps. 29:1; 89:7; Dan. 3:25, 28.

[150] See also Die Sagen der Juden. I, by Josef bin Gorion, and Etudes by J. lagrange.

[151] See the book Rephaim by Dr. P. Karge.

[152] See also Les Monuments Megalithiques de Palestine in the Archives De L'Institut De Paleontologie Humaine, 1935 by Stekelis. He ascribes these monuments to the Ghassulians, a people who lived some 4,000 years before Jesus Christ. See also Cultes, Mythes, et Religions, by Reinach.

[153] See Ex. 31:13; Lev 19:3, 30; 23:15, 38; 25:8 (twice); 26:2, 34, 35, 43; 1 Chron. 23:31; 2 Chron. 2:4; 8:13; 31:3; 36:21; Neh. 10:33; Isa 56:4; Eze. 20:12, 13, 16, 19, 21, 24; 22:8, 26; 23:38; 44:24; 45:17; 46:3.

[154] If one is wondering whether a free-will offering was not required every week, the answer is in the negative. The reference here is to the prescriptions of Deut. 16:10 addressed to the Jews: during the feast of the seven weeks they had to contribute an offering. Paul asks that these annual offerings be gathered before he comes, 1 Cor. 16:2.

[155] Born again, "child of God," but not yet justified.

[156] "Son" of God, justified, new creature.

www.ingramcontent.com/pod-product-compliance
Lightning Source LLC
Chambersburg PA
CBHW071553040426
42452CB00008B/1161